POMPEY'S GENTLEMAN JIM

POMPEY'S GENTLEMAN JIM

Peter Jeffs

Breedon Books Sport

First published in Great Britain by
The Breedon Books Publishing Company Limited
45 Friar Gate, Derby DE1 1DA
1988

ISBN 0 907969 45 3

Printed by Billing & Sons Limited, Hylton Road, Worcester.
Jacket designed by Graham Hales

Photographic Credits

Photographs supplied by BBC Hulton Picture Library, Colorsport,
Mrs Ann Dickinson, Keystone Picture Agency, *The News*, Portsmouth.

Contents

Acknowledgements

THIS book could not have been written without the full co-operation of Mrs Ann Dickinson and Mrs Myrtle Bone and the many busy people who found time to talk to me about their various associations with Jimmy Dickinson and who provided reminiscences and source material. The following have my grateful thanks: David Barber of the Football Association, Mike Barnard, Keith Blackburn, Gary Chalk, Len Curtis, Peter Harris, Gordon Jeffery, Eddie Lever, Mick Mellows, Mike Neasom of *The News* (Portsmouth), John Phillips, Len Phillips, Barbara Powe, Tony Pullein of *Football Monthly*, Len Robson, Doug Rumbold, Don Smith, Leslie Spink, Mr & Mrs George White, Ros Wilson, Sir Walter Winterbottom CBE and Mickie Worthington.

I was glad of the assistance of the Portsmouth Central Library staff, the office staff of Portsmouth Football Club and Fiona Cooper and *The News* (Portsmouth) Photo Library. The continued help and encouragement of Mick Cooper, the co-author of *Pompey — The History of Portsmouth Football Club* and the access which he provided to his notes and statistics was invaluable.

Foreword by
Tom Finney OBE, JP

I HAVE had many happy recollections of Jimmy Dickinson with the England team. He was a very quiet, modest man and immensely loyal, extremely fit — in fact, the ideal professional footballer.

I played with and against Jimmy on many occasions and always enjoyed my tussles with him. I was assured of a hard and fair game against a great player who had craft and skill in abundance.

He would have been an outstanding player in any era, a great credit to the game, and his loyalty, sportsmanship and dedication are sadly missed by us all.

INTRODUCTION

JIMMY Dickinson was unique. Unique for his loyalty to the game of soccer and to Portsmouth Football Club. The quiet, unassuming man was synonymous with Pompey — the club he loved. Indeed, Pompey was *his* club.

When he died on that Monday afternoon six years ago, in his favourite chair, in Alton where he had lived all his life, the legend was born. The legend of his service to Pompey, to his country and to the game itself. Of the example he set to his generation and the next, of his humility and, above all, of his dignity.

His record is now legendary, not only in Britain but beyond. The biography of such a man cannot avoid being eulogistic and for this no apologies are tendered. Pick up any book on soccer records and Jimmy Dickinson's name is there. For the record he played his 764th and last Football League game in April 1965, on his 40th birthday and for his only club. This record has subsequently been surpassed by only one player — John Trollope of Swindon Town, who made 770 appearances between 1960 and 1980. In seven seasons, including three consecutive campaigns from 1961 to 1964, Jimmy Dickinson never missed a League game. He won two Football League Championship medals and a Third Division championship medal, but twice suffered the pain of the club's relegation.

He played 48 times for England and his international career took him to the 1950 and 1954 World Cup Finals, to practically every European country, to South America three times and to the United States. All but three of his caps were won at left-half and only Bobby Moore made more appearances for England in that position. Dickinson enjoyed a run of 25 consecutive matches for his country. He finished on the losing side on only ten occasions in his 48 matches, England winning 27 of them.

Alas, his skills have not been recorded on film. They are images which can be recalled only by the memories of those who saw him play; similarly, his accomplishments are recorded only through the written word. Most professional footballers, even some of those who have made an outstanding contribution to the game, are forgotten once their playing days are over. From time to time their names are the subject of reminiscence but, 20 years on, they do not generally make news value. Success in the football world is more than usually ephemeral.

Today, Jimmy Dickinson can be held as a shining example of the heights which soccer and its players can reach, as the epitome of the real professional player. Heights that many a modern player could never aspire to, professionalism which has lost its meaning in the modern game. He was probably the last of those who loved their football and their club far more than any reward.

Dickinson's love of the game transcended asking for a transfer, protesting about this or that, or demanding to know what the future was to bring. This is the age of the football mercenary, of the transfer request, of freedom of contract, of huge signing-on fees with loyalty barely extending as far as the length of the present contract.

As far as the modern game was concerned, Jimmy Dickinson was hurt when it was brought into disrepute, particularly if its image was damaged by players or managers. He found the modern trend for 'lifting the lid' on dressing-room incidents and tensions — which are inevitable in any club and in any era — particularly distasteful. As he once commented, "I suppose if anyone could have cashed in by selling his memories, then I could have done. I've been in the game a long time and in those years there have been plenty of incidents which would have made tasty reading. But that would have been a poor way of repaying all the pleasure and satisfaction the game has given me."

A biography of a man such as Jimmy Dickinson could serve the sole purpose of entertaining only the fervent football follower and the supporters of Portsmouth Football Club in particular. But that would not be the whole story. His style and approach to the game was sufficiently creditable to warrant inspection as a fine example of sportsmanship, not only to football but also to the whole of the sporting world. He held the record, now inconceivable, of never being cautioned by a referee in the whole of his career. His contemporaries recall that if Jimmy Dickinson ever accidentally tripped an opponent, they could swear that he blushed with embarrassment.

It could be argued that in Dickinson's time football was at a peak but, conversely, not subject to the commercial pressures of the modern game which, if applied to any sport, pollute the spirit of true sportsmanship on and off the field. This was not an ugly age as now — not one of violence and abuse.

Sport raises passions to a dangerous degree, often because of the far wider loyalties for which it acts as a focus. Professional sportsmen represent their followers at local or international level and their deeds are often recorded in heroic terms. In peacetime they can carry a nation's or a city's hopes in a manner similar to soldiers at war. It is little wonder that sportsmen doing battle on their own and others' behalf, get carried away. It has never been more important that those whom we admire on the field should perform their feats within the rules of their particular game and even within the laws of the land.

Not that players or spectators were any less committed in Jimmy Dickinson's time — not that Dickinson or his contemporaries had any less of a will to win. It was still a man's game and Jimmy Dickinson proved that it is possible to play it hard but scrupulously fair — there was never a player in the country waiting to settle an old score with him — not even after 700 games.

He was one of the most talented and respected players of his age and was a peerless left-half — and he was more than that. He had spirit, courage and determination. He was never half-hearted, he literally never gave up. His commitment was total to his club and country and he was profoundly patriotic.

Had he been able to display his many qualities in the football scene of today, not only would his fame have been more established but also his fortune. The bulk of Dickinson's career was played within the constraints of the 'maximum wage' structure. In these days, with his First Division and international honours, his talent would be monitored by the media and exploited very successfully through the various commercial channels. Curiously, there might have been even more of a market in the early 1950s, with massive crowds and the sports-hungry public of those so called 'golden days' of soccer.

Jimmy Dickinson was almost a perfectionist as far as his playing performance was concerned, whether it was as a professional footballer or relaxing at tennis, cricket, golf or swimming. His outstanding record of performances over some 20 seasons can largely be attributed to extraordinary physical strength which enabled him to absorb bruises and knocks and the heavy demands of the League season and often a summer with England for good measure. It was a testament to his outstanding stamina, coupled with his effort to control his weight and fitness, that he was playing at wing-half in the Second Division at 38 years of age.

How did he stay the course for so long? The value of his enthusiasm for playing the game for its own sake and his sensible life-style cannot be over-estimated. He was a dedicated, conscientious trainer — albeit that training was less intensive than today, except for the time when Pompey's footballers were under the 'command' of George Smith in the twilight of Dickinson's career.

In truth, Jimmy Dickinson rarely excited; he just did the obvious thing superbly well. His play rarely raised a howl or the temperature. His strengths were simply his fine anticipation, distribution of the ball and,

above all, his tackling. So clean, so incisive and so beautifully-timed. His play was like his personality — quiet, strong and effective. His game was straightforward, reliable with no frills. At international level he simply did as he was told, consistently, in a defensive role. Under an international team manager such as Walter Winterbottom, who pursued his coaching and tactical theories with almost religious application, this was a prime essential.

There was no flamboyance and a minimum of ostentation. Dickinson's manner was understated and self-contained and he was rarely in the news except for his performances on the field. He rarely swore and if he permitted himself some mild profanity in the heat of the moment, it was invariably followed by a self-conscious apology.

Jimmy Dickinson did not like to be seen to be angry himself and was upset if any of his fellow players quarrelled. On the field there were no histrionics — if things went wrong he would shake his head disdainfully. There was no word of complaint, he simply got on with the game.

He found it hard to answer questions about himself. Not that he was inarticulate, it was just that there was a natural diffidence in him. There was none of the spontaneity of the extrovert games player. His dry, whimsical humour was popular in the dressing-room. He liked a joke and no one could ever have called him narrow-minded, but he would discreetly withdraw from the conversation at the peaks of collective ribaldry.

By nature he was mild-mannered, retiring, home-loving. He was certainly not one of those of his profession who lapped up the social life which the 'hangers-on' love to provide. By his own admission, he was never affected by the size or support of any crowd, other than once or twice very early in his career. He gave his all whether the attendance was counted in hundreds or in tens of thousands. Off the field he would avoid crowds where possible and was almost shy of meeting supporters and signing autographs.

The country atmosphere of Alton, where he was born and bred and where he made his home with his wife Ann, suited Jimmy. He was only too happy to make the 60-mile round trip to Fratton Park each day and then, training over, slip away and leave the other players to soak up the fame, recognition and social life in and around Portsmouth, while he might enjoy a quiet drink in his local with perhaps a close friend for company.

Jimmy Dickinson thought a great deal about football and he had a retentive memory of past games and players. A characteristic of all great men is their attention to detail. With his intellectual approach, Dickinson had a fine grasp of tactics and possessed firm ideas of how football should be played. Not that he was a great contributor to dressing-room discussions, his reticence restricting his views often to a mere aside to a colleague. Like many of his contemporaries, he had little time for coaching theories and, whilst retaining a respect for Walter Winterbottom, felt that an international player should be left alone without the need for individual coaching at that stage in his career.

The following chapters will attempt to describe a career of service to the game, on and off the field, and to analyse those characteristics which made Jimmy Dickinson such a paragon of honesty, loyalty and dignity through the peaks and troughs of Pompey's post-war seasons. This is not intended to be a chronicle of the 'good old days' because, for so long, Jimmy Dickinson worked on and off the field to halt the club's decline. As club secretary, for instance, he could only watch helplessly as Pompey teetered on the brink of the abyss of financial ruin and extinction. And in the most desperate times, the club turned to Jimmy Dickinson as the most unlikely stopgap emergency manager ever.

Although he knew the great days of Pompey success in the early 1950s and, as an England international, toured the world and sampled high tension at the World Cup Finals, by his own admission his greatest thrills were to lead Portsmouth to the Third Division championship in 1961-2 and to see the club saved from relegation back to the Third Division in his last game of all, on his 40th Birthday.

In his roles as public relations officer, an eminently suitable appointment for one so friendly, club secretary for many years, manager and briefly chief executive, Jimmy Dickinson was always held in awe and respect. His very name carried weight in and around the city of Portsmouth and could have carried even more weight to his and the club's advantage but for his retiring nature. Yet, despite such natural reticence, he was always prepared to greet visitors at Fratton Park when they particularly asked to meet him, even when his time was at a premium. He was ever friendly and conscious of the club's duty to its public.

Peter Jeffs
August 1988

Those who saw him in his prime will remember the tall, lean, wiry build, the head held high, the bowed footballer's legs and the rolling sailor's gait. They will recall the open face, the short-back-and-sides haircut with the orderly quiff. Most appealingly, they will also recall the happy smile above those honest grey eyes. Above all, if you were lucky enough to be one of the few who knew him intimately, you could not fail to be struck by how unaware he was of his greatness as a player or a man.

His life was devoted to football. If Jimmy Dickinson had lived, then he may have been retired by now but, unlike many of his playing colleagues who became disaffected towards the club, he would not have been able to stay away from Fratton Park. He would have wanted to serve Pompey in any capacity, however humble. Football and its people were — and always would have been — his life.

How happy he would have been to see his club back in the First Division — like all those who really cared for the club, that was a dream he cherished most.

Portsmouth is a city of famous names and its football club will have no prouder claim than that its most famous player was Jimmy Dickinson, a man who served football as eminently as any who played the game. His record as a great player and clubman will emphasize the significance of his individual contribution to a sporting activity which mirrors and has become an integral part of our life and our culture.

As 'Linesman' of the *Portsmouth Evening News* wrote on Jimmy Dickinson's playing retirement after 21 years, "Just a few players of supreme ability write a personal chapter in the history of a club and Dickinson is one of those soccer greats."

CHILDHOOD, BOYHOOD AND DISCOVERY

Above: The eight-year-old with his boxing trophies.

Below: Alton Boxing Club with young 'Boy Dickinson' in the centre.

T HE doleful tolling of the school bell pierced the cold of the winter's morning and announced the first welcome break of the day for the boys of Alton Senior Boys' School. Almost immediately a shouting, jostling throng of pupils burst into the playground intent on making the most of their 15 minutes' freedom and indulging their passion for football.

It could hardly be called a match — that implies an element of organisation and preparation. It was just a 'kick-around' and the boys fell into teams with a lack of fuss and formality that would have mystified their peers. Coats and jackets were discarded to form makeshift goalposts, a scuffed, worn tennis-ball was produced and battle commenced. Anybody who wanted to join in could do so and usually did.

For the young master on his very first day at the Alton school it was a chance to have a stroll around and find his bearings; to breath a sigh of relief after the ordeal of his first period as a form teacher in his new career. His love of football was bound to draw his attention to the young lads parading, even showing off, their skills in the corner of the playground. One boy immediately took his eye — and not because he was the smallest and possibly the youngest in the pack. The teacher was Eddie Lever, who recalled, "At eight years of age he made the big lads of 13 and 14 look silly." The youngster's skill on the ball that morning, coupled with his being so quick and alert, thrilled Lever, a former Portsmouth professional player, and prompted him to enquire, "What's your name, son?" Back came the reply, "Jimmy Dickinson, sir." A relationship and a bond which was to last a lifetime had been formed, albeit tentatively, that February morning in 1934.

Greatness in sport begins early. True greatness in a sport — that state of performing on a plane clearly higher than your fellows — always begins in childhood. We can see the significance of that beginning by a backward look at how and where it took place.

James William Dickinson was born during the early morning of Friday, 24 April 1925, at the family home at 6 Tower Street, Alton, in north east Hampshire towards the Surrey border. He was the third child of Harry and Alice Dickinson and their only son after six years of marriage, with his father then 34 years of age and his mother one year younger. The family was completed by his two sisters, Myrtle and Beryl, who were five and two years old respectively at his birth.

Alton, set amid the wooded stretches, open downs and pastoral vales in that valley of the River Wey, was then a small country town of approximately 5,000 souls. An agricultural district, it was centred around the farming community — its crops, its cattle and the product of its hops. The brewing industry was the main employer in the charming Georgian market town which later grew as a residential town with the addition of 20th century industries. This early environment, with its fierce independence and close community spirit, was to be crucial in the formation of the character of 'young James'. His village childhood would remain in his memory as an intensely happy period of his life and forge an affinity with the town where he was to live and die.

Jimmy's birth was the day before the Jubilee FA Cup Final at Wembley, where Sheffield United beat Cardiff City on the same afternoon as Portsmouth drew at Clapton Orient to finish fourth in the Second Division that 1924-5 season. For one who was to be such a patriot and proud wearer of an England shirt in the years to come, it was perhaps apt that St George's Day should be celebrated around the date of his birth.

Alton's main claim to fame, other than being the location of the cruel murder of the child 'Sweet' Fanny Adams — from where the expression arose — in 1867, lay within the Chawton area where Jane Austen lived in a brick house, now restored and open to the public.

At the time of Jimmy's birth, Britain lived under Prime Minister Stanley Baldwin with chronic unemployment as a condition of solvency. Class antagonism was fuelled by a decade of vigorous social life for the well-to-do. The General Strike, the climax to years of industrial unrest, was a year ahead and the impending Depression, set off by the Wall Street Crash of 1929, was part of a world slump more far reaching than any other recession before or since.

The first commercial phonograph records were sold that month in 1925 and within weeks, John Logie Baird was to send the first television transmission of a moving picture image across his room. Such luxuries were far from the minds of the Dickinson family that year as, like any working-class family, they struggled to survive, in their case on the 30 shillings per week from Harry's employment with a local steam traction company, employment which he sustained despite continuous ill-health as an asthmatic. Harry's company specialised in ploughing and threshing on farms, clearing lakes and ponds and making roads. Their equipment, worked by steam engines and steam rollers, was a well-known sight in the area and, from an

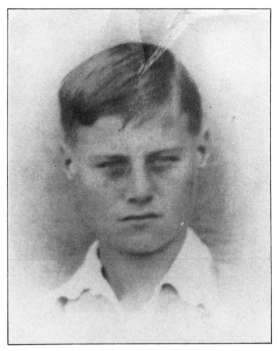

Above: An early school portrait.
Below: The boy becomes a young teenager.

The proud member of the school team under Eddie Lever.

early age, Jimmy would enjoy the days out on the roads and in the fields, riding on the engines, excited by the heat, the steam and the noise.

Harry's health, which had already caused him to miss active service in World War One, was a constant source of concern. His one sporting interest, albeit non-participating, was boxing. His son was still at a tender age when Harry introduced him to the Alton Boxing Club, putting him under the care of a former professional boxer, Jock Baggaley, the club coach. With his stamina and sharp reactions, Jimmy was soon more than a match for other boys of seven or eight, despite his lack of inches at that stage.

So it was that the young boy, who was to grow into a gentle, dignified adult, first found fame in Alton as a junior boxer. In 1936, at the age of ten, 'Midget' Dickinson at five-stone was presenting the local boxing club committee with some difficulty as they tried to find a match for him in their tournaments. The *Hampshire Herald* subsequently reported that the local 'embryo champion Boy Dickinson' was eventually matched against a bigger opponent but by virtue of his footwork and speed was awarded the contest as the more nimble boxer.

His reputation in local boxing circles continued to grow and by the time he was 12, Jimmy was invited to compete in a major tournament in Alton. In the first bout on that programme in November 1937, which also included several amateur champions from all over the country, he fought one Len Benson in a four-round contest and was defeated after a plucky fight. The strength of the heavier Benson told but it is clear that 'Boy Dickinson' gave him several trying moments with his fast footwork. The enthusiastic crowd and later local newspaper reports gave full credit to such a young lad for his courage when obviously smaller and of lighter build.

Jimmy's mother steadfastly opposed her husband's hopes of a boxing career for her young son who was 'the apple of her eye'. On Harry Dickinson's death she was to successfully steer him away from the boxing club and into outdoor pursuits, particularly football.

Although he was unashamedly fussed over by his mother and two older sisters, the quiet young lad's upbringing in the family's modest two-bedroom semi-detached was unexceptional and could be paralleled by hundreds of boys in rural Hampshire. What was unusual was his early and total obsession with sports of all kinds, allied with his stamina and fitness.

Jimmy once recalled his first organised game of football when he was only five years old. "I shall never forget that match. I'd just been given my first pair of football boots for Christmas and the game was between boys from either end of town. I was only a little chap but, wearing those new boots, I thought I could hold my own with anyone. I couldn't, of course, but if nothing else, my first game did teach me to take knocks without complaining."

Primary education at All Saints' School in Queen's Road started almost at the same time as the Dickinsons were moving to 13 Bow Street 'just around the corner' to take care of Jimmy's grandfather in the last years of his life. This was to be Jimmy's home for almost 25 years until the time of his marriage.

Anything other than games did not warrant much attention at school but the education was traditional and typically of basic soundness. The early move to Alton Senior Boys' School meant that Jimmy, like many an Altonian, was brought up in somewhat Dickensian conditions with the three R's — reading, 'riting and 'rithmatic — as the main subjects. Jimmy's later modest admission that he was 'quite reasonable' at his lessons do not do justice to his academic prowess, which was clearly above average.

Inevitably, Jimmy performed in most sports with distinction and was quite simply a 'natural' at all ball games. He boxed at school and the timing and anticipation which were to be the hallmarks of his professional career had their roots in that early boxing coaching. Jimmy was the star of the school athletics team, competing with great success each year in the annual sports day — one year sweeping the board by winning the half-mile, quarter-mile, 220 yards and 100 yards on the same day. Old school friends remember his outstanding stamina — and always that inordinate modesty in victory.

More significantly, at 14 Jimmy took up tennis and at weekends would enjoy many a game with his pals. Within a few years he had blossomed into a fine player who, with later coaching, reached county standard with Hampshire. Tennis and cricket were always to retain his interest and over the years, he would make his annual pilgrimage to Wimbledon for the Finals. In common with a large number of professional footballers he was to take up golf and, with a 12-handicap, would welcome the chance, after training at the football club, to travel out to a country club course for a relaxing round.

In his early teens his football skills flourished under the coaching of Eddie Lever, his school games master. From that time on, Lever was to be singularly responsible for Jimmy Dickinson's development as a player, not least as a result of his forming and leading the Alton Youth Club based at the school.

Lever, born in Burnopfield on Tyneside, joined Portsmouth FC at the age of 17 and the club agreed to him continuing his studies to qualify as a teacher. He played in the Reserves for some years before joining Aldershot, where his career ended in 1934 because of a troublesome cartilage in his knee. Coincidentally, whilst gaining his teaching diploma at Chester College, Lever was a close friend and class-mate of Walter Winterbottom, later to become the first FA Director of Coaching and England team manager during Jimmy Dickinson's international career.

On his return to teaching, with mathematics his speciality, Lever secured the post at Alton and with his love of the game, and more particularly his high regard for Jack Tinn and the Portsmouth club who had been so considerate of his future at the time of his injury, he continued to scout for young talent. Young Jimmy Dickinson's potential was apparent to him that very first day at the school and Lever took Jimmy under his wing and made a point of giving him regular coaching. "He simply lapped up any tips I gave him," Eddie Lever remembers to this day.

Jimmy was naturally left-footed but typically made sure he learned to use his right foot. His greatest ambition was to make the school football team and, sure enough, at age nine he was picked at outside-left. With the average age of the team at 13 or 14, he had cause to feel pretty pleased with himself. It was enough to persuade his father to play 'head tennis' with a balloon in the front room in an effort to improve his heading ability as a compensation for his lack of inches in height.

The school had their best-ever team and Jimmy Dickinson and his friend Stan Earl, who was to make his mark with Leyton Orient after a spell at Portsmouth, were to graduate to the professional ranks.

It was taken for granted that Jimmy would leave school in 1939, at the customary age of 14, after an education which was functional and without frills. Jimmy is remembered by Eddie Lever as a bright and intelligent lad, well served by the system then in being. He never really aspired to higher education, primarily because he loved his sport too much to waste time on study and because the family was in some need of a further bread-winner.

Alton's long association with the brewing industry meant that a school-leaver tended to find work in one of the two breweries in town which employed literally hundreds of local people. Courage's Brewery in nearby Turf Street was sufficiently impressed by Jimmy's school reference to offer the smart, well-spoken but retiring youngster a job, with reasonable prospects of advancement, as a costing clerk.

No sooner had he settled into his new job than the twin blows of his dear father's death and the outbreak of war hit him. Jimmy Dickinson threw himself into the activities of the youth club and the close friendship of his pals. The 'gang' managed to fit in three visits per week to the local cinema, timed to coincide with the regular change of film, and a session at the milk-bar down the road beforehand. Physical training in the youth club gym twice a week, countless games of table-tennis and the regular dances, when Eddie Lever played the piano whilst the youngster rather self-consciously took to the floor, took up all his time. He even managed to fit in time for boxing, albeit limited to coaching youngsters in his mother's back garden.

The outbreak of war brought to Alton, like everywhere else, the blackouts, the air-raid shelters, the wail of sirens and a shortage of consumer goods. As far as Jimmy and his pals were concerned, the closing of the cinema and the occasional cancellation of football matches for fear of air-raids were the main sources of irritation. The lads became used to seeing troops in the town as soldiers from all over the world were billeted in many homes.

For all that, Jimmy's life centred largely around his football and the youth club team. Eddie Lever coached indoors during the week and played behind Jimmy at wing-half in the Saturday matches as something of an 'over-age' player. This was crucial to the youngsters' development

The Alton Youth Club forward line on parade.

and inside-left Jimmy Dickinson became a prolific goalscorer. Later in his career he showed neither inclination nor aptitude for scoring goals, but those 1941-2 records show 57 goals from 35 matches in local football.

Playing equipment was often a problem and, in the absence of a set of shirts, it was decided to play in white — simply because any old white shirt would suffice. A variety of shorts and stockings decorated the team but there was nothing casual about the regular, keenly contested games against locally-based military teams and Jimmy would later remember with relish the 'battle royals' with the nearby Royal Engineers. Such teams invariably included players of varying pre-war Football League experience and an Alton team would often provide the opposition for star-studded Army sides in support of various war charities.

At the age of fifteen at inside left in the brewery works team.

A particular thrill for the 16-year-old Dickinson was to be part of an Alton team playing an Army XI for the 'Red Cross Aid to Russia' fund on 10 December 1941. His outside-left partner that afternoon was Sergeant-Instructor Compton, better known as Denis Compton, then of Arsenal, who was guesting for the town side. The Army team included such players as Tommy Lawton of

Everton and England and Jimmy Hagan of Sheffield United.

Such matches were virtually a matter of grown men pitted against teenagers but the youth club lads, by virtue of Eddie Lever's forceful coaching, stood up well to the challenges. Jimmy's physical presence — he was taking after his father for height and build — was a great asset and it was clear that he was growing and developing in stature, both mentally and physically, as the 'man of the house'.

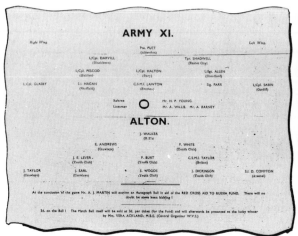

The line-up from the programme with the left-wing partnership for Alton of Dickinson and Compton playing in aid of the Red Cross to Russia Fund.

Eddie Lever could wait no longer to introduce his protégé to Portsmouth and by the end of that season he had written to Jack Tinn, then Pompey manager, in the first of his attempts to convince Tinn to give Dickinson a trial. Lever drove him to Portsmouth for one of the Sunday morning trials which the club staged on local pitches for young hopefuls. Whatever impression the shy, well-built teenager from Alton made, it was insufficient to make Jack Tinn follow up Lever's strong almost insistent recommendation.

The next season it was back to youth club and works football for Jimmy Dickinson until yet another of the War Fund matches proved to be the springboard for what Lever saw as his inevitable jump into professional football. The Army team, full of experienced League players, included the Wolves full-back George Taylor, who wasted no time in passing a strong message to Major Frank Buckley, the manager at Molineux, about the impressive Alton youngster. When Lever received a letter from Wolves, seeking permission to sign Jimmy Dickinson, it brought matters to a head.

Whether young Jimmy, or his mother and sisters for that matter, would have relished the prospect of his moving to the Midlands in such circumstances and in such uncertain times is irrelevant. Lever refused the approach outright and even went so far as to add a rider that, if Dickinson was to join any club, then it would be Pompey.

Eddie Lever, Dickinson's schoolmaster, youth club leader and mentor.

for Pompey as an amateur in the unreal world of wartime football. His very first visit to Fratton Park — all his football had been played in the Alton district until that day — for the meaningless end-of-season friendly match against Reading was marked by a 4-2 victory for the home side. Jimmy was listed as 'G.W.Dickinson' in the programme which also showed five guest players for Pompey, including the talented Ernie Taylor from Newcastle United.

It was a nervous start for Jimmy Dickinson but the local Alton newspaper reported that 'some of those flicks soon got the eye of the large crowd'. His debut was not helped by his having to mark Jimmy Hagan, who was guesting for Reading. He had encountered Hagan before, as we have noted, but this time he found the Sheffield United man difficult to contain. Dickinson remarked later, "I soon began to understand that there was a lot I didn't know about football. If nothing else that day, Jimmy Hagan taught me never to give up hope."

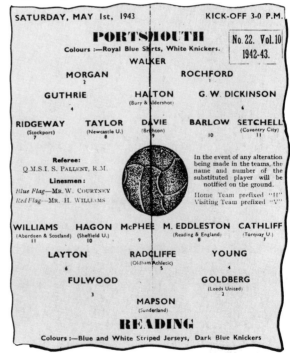

The line-up in the programme for Dickinson's first match for Pompey – shown as G.W.Dickinson at number 6.

'The Ranger', then the *Portsmouth Evening News* reporter, was moved to comment on Eddie Lever's discovery that "it looks as if he has put Jack Tinn on to something good". What a glorious understatement that proved to be.

Jimmy Dickinson never really harboured any dreams of taking up football for a living. Typically, he hoped for no more than to play as an amateur in a high grade. He did not follow the League game and its stars and had

By the same post another letter was on its way to Jack Tinn. Did he realise that Wolves were after the lad that he continued to ignore? Lever really was insistent this time — bluffing that if Tinn would not sign him, then Lever would encourage Dickinson to join the Midlands club. Tinn telephoned him at school the next day, confirming that a place would be found for Jimmy Dickinson in the Pompey team the following Saturday, the last day of the 1942-3 season.

So it was that the 18-year-old, now five feet ten inches and approaching twelve stone, made his first appearance

only seen one professional game. A cousin took him to a match at nearby Aldershot, when the mighty Arsenal were the opposition, but Jimmy was singularly unimpressed. He had a good office job in the brewery with reasonable prospects, was due to be called up for National Service the following year and then intended to go back to his old job. He saw professional football as something of a dead-end job — there was no glamorous image attached to the game at that time, or rewards to match.

Nevertheless, he was thrilled at the recognition of his ability and Eddie Lever's firm belief in his capabilities encouraged him to pursue the chance of a career in football. His mother, in her quiet way, and his two sisters were obviously proud of 'young James'. Beryl, to Jimmy's amusement, proceeded to start a scrapbook of his press-cuttings.

The following 1943-4 season saw professional football kept alive only with great difficulty. The competitions, on a regional basis, were a pale imitation of the real thing, but the Government was aware of football's value as a distraction and morale-booster to the civilian population. The 'call-up' of players for war service — both military and in munitions — was biting hard into the resources of every club and they experienced difficulty in fielding sides of acceptable quality.

A loudspeaker appeal for spectators to make up the teams was not unusual and many were the old-timers who emerged from retirement to 'make up the numbers'. With most of the male population of footballing age in the Armed Services, or working long shifts in industry, no club could expect to field a complete team of their signed professionals. So 'guest players' were permitted, much to the delight of clubs like Aldershot who enjoyed their best side ever during the war because of the large military encampment in the town. The Shots often paraded a full team of guests, sometimes sides of international standard. Many stars, including the complete England half-back line of Cliff Britton, Stan Cullis and Joe Mercer, were seen in the appropriate red, white and blue of the Aldershot 'Soldiers'.

Most clubs were not so lucky. Brighton, when they had to fulfil a Christmas Day fixture at Norwich, travelled with only five players. They completed their team from soldiers in the crowd and went down 18-0.

Jimmy Dickinson's early involvement with Pompey was restricted to training twice weekly in the evening, rail travel permitting. He waited patiently until 11 December 1943 for his debut in the War League South, at home to Chelsea. The spurious regional competition attracted little interest other than as a pleasant diversion from the rigours of wartime England. Conditions were often dismal and difficult but a crowd of 4,780 at Fratton Park watched quietly as Pompey slipped to a 5-1 defeat. Rochford was missing through injury and the regular left-half, Summerbee, moved to left-back in his place, thus creating room for Dickinson. He took his chance in style and 'The Ranger' described the newcomer as 'strong without being boisterous, he never shirks a tackle, invariably gets there and he knows what to do with the ball when he gets it'. It was a concise and simple commentary on Jimmy Dickinson's play — and was just as apt after he became

Captain of England. Jimmy Dickinson leads his country in an ATC international.

18

an experienced international as when he was an untried amateur.

After a further four games, during which time Pompey lost 6-3 at Southampton on Christmas Day 1943 and then defeated their local rivals 4-2 at Fratton Park two days later, Jack Tinn had seen enough of the Alton teenager to offer him professional terms. Jimmy Dickinson signed the forms on Saturday, 8 January 1944, immediately before Pompey's match at Aldershot. Portsmouth lost 3-2 in a game which saw Stan Cullis and Reg Flewin — the current England centre-half and the future England number-five respectively — on opposing sides. In his quiet way Flewin, as Pompey's captain, nursed Dickinson through those early matches and their understanding of each other's play in defence was to be a crucial factor in the club's post-war successes.

At this time Jimmy Dickinson was not yet 19 years of age and the excitement which he felt at his elevation into the professional ranks was tempered by the prospect of National Service within a few months and possible acceptance for RAF aircrew. With an eye to that future and with his usual thriftiness, the £10 signing-on fee from Pompey at once went into the bank.

His involvement with the Air Training Corps, for whom he volunteered in December 1941 along with his Alton youth club pals, provided more football and later some national recognition which was to enhance his reputation. He became involved with the training for no better reason than it filled another evening per week and was conveniently under the same roof as the youth club at his old school, where he spent all of his leisure time anyway. Training was provided for all branches of the RAF but particularly for potential aircrew.

Cadet Corporal Dickinson was soon representing the Alton Squadron and then the South-Eastern Command on the football field. National recognition came on 15 April 1944 when boys of the ATC met in an international match for the first time. Jimmy Dickinson, as the only cadet with professional status, was the natural choice to captain the England team against Scotland at Shawfield Park, Glasgow, the home of Clyde FC. The crowd of 7,000 saw England win 2-0. The first goal, from a corner kick, was a perfectly-timed header from Jimmy Dickinson, the game's outstanding player. His display prompted the Air Marshall ATC to write and congratulate him, "Your personal performance will be remembered by all who witnessed the game."

The Scottish football correspondents were not slow to recognise Dickinson's qualities and in their rave notices were comparing him with his senior counterpart, Joe Mercer. One columnist wrote, "The curl in his legs is not the only point of resemblance — this boy is certain to be seen in the bigger game at Hampden or Wembley one day not too distant."

Two weeks later, Portsmouth's last match of the season, against Brentford, was marked by the visit of General Montgomery, the president of Pompey, and the rare display of the FA Cup still held by the club after their win at Wembley five years previously to the day.

Above: The young sailor on National Service

Below: Jack Tinn – finally gave Dickinson his chance after Lever's insistence.

In later years, Jimmy Dickinson was to be a firm favourite of 'Monty's', more particularly after the war hero had retired and made his home close to Alton. Dickinson would often be mentioned in dispatches from 'Monty' to post-war Pompey managers. One such set of instructions to Eddie Lever in the early 1950s ended typically, "Tell Dickinson it is captaincy that counts in war and in football, lead the team well and they should never lose."

The brief appearance of the FA Cup prompted the General to enquire of manager Jack Tinn where it was kept in such secrecy. There was considerable amusement when Tinn assured him that in football circles that was as closely-guarded a secret as the date of the opening of the Second Front.

Secretary-manager Tinn made a big impression on Dickinson, who later recalled,"I was fortunate in coming under a manager like Jack Tinn, one of the most understanding and human men I have ever met." Tinn had been steeped in football all his life in the North-East but it was not until after World War One that he took up his first managership, at South Shields. Pompey were attracted by his reputation as one of the finest judges of a player in the game. It was said of him in those early days that "Jack Tinn could buy players with old tramcar tickets and sell them for thousands of pounds".

Tinn was recruited as manager in 1927 and his 20-year autocratic reign at Fratton Park led to three Wembley Cup Finals, in 1929, 1934 and 1939. The latter proved 'third time lucky' with the historic victory over Wolves and the creation of the legend of Tinn's lucky white spats.

The spats, flaunted on match days, were about all the players saw of the manager because training and tactics were largely in the hands of the trainers and the experienced players. Dickinson would recall the human touches but above all the awe and the remoteness — the 'god' in the office whom players approached with trepidation.

The style of management was just as authoritarian as that which had prevailed throughout the inter-war period. The manager was a distant figure in the chain of command and Jimmy Dickinson kept his distance and knew his station, even with the old hands in the team. There was certainly no room for 'concensus football' in those days. Football, both on and off the field, was in the hands of shrewd, often experienced directors who controlled key areas of team selection and player transfers, with the manager more of a figurehead. Such power as was held by directors in those days is often today in the hands of club-owning chairmen.

Jimmy Dickinson, meanwhile, the quiet lad, so inoffensive off the field, was blossoming into a mature, almost assertive young player on the pitch. With his conscientiousness in training and his willingness to listen to the old professionals, still there from the 1939 Cup-winning side, things augured well for his future. He remembered fondly that men like Reg Flewin and Cliff Parker "never hesitated to give me and the other youngsters the benefit of their experience."

The imminent threat of National Service still hung over Dickinson and his anxious wait to be called-up was not helped by his being somewhat 'messed about' by the RAF. As a member of the ATC, he had been provisionally accepted for aircrew in the pilot-navigator category on a 'deferred service' basis but, after a tortuous wait of ten months, he was finally notified that the RAF had no use for him and he was discharged, for no apparent reason.

During the wait he was able to see out the rest of that 1943-4 season, playing in 13 of the remaining 15 matches and welcoming the emergence of Peter Harris to the Pompey scene after he, too, had been a part of those regular evening training sessions for promising amateurs. The two lads, of such similar demeanour and reticence, were to become key figures in Pompey's post-war successes and close companions in the Fratton dressing-room.

Jack Tinn was becoming anxious that his rising star should see out his National Service as close to home as possible so that Dickinson would continue to be available to play. Jimmy now had a leaning towards the Royal Marines but, after some prompting from Tinn, finally plumped for the Royal Navy with the false notion, possibly suggested by Tinn, that one had to do some service in the Navy before being considered by the Marines.

Ordinary Seaman Dickinson JW, JX 723508 joined the Royal Navy on 15 August 1944 and the records show the 19-year-old as a strapping 5ft 10ins tall with a 36-inch chest. A run-down converted Butlin's holiday camp at Skegness was his first 'port of call', with accommodation in chalets for two weeks under the auspices of the shore

establishment HMS Royal Arthur, where he suffered the rigours of what is known as basic training. All servicemen will be familiar with the recipe — square-bashing, PT and then more of the same.

The shore establishment HMS Glendower, based at Pwllheli in North Wales, was the centre where Dickinson received his basic seamanship training for three months, again in the same sort of holiday chalets.

A welcome spot of leave and a telephone call to Jack Tinn enabled him to make his first appearance of the 1944-5 season at Brentford where Pompey were, as the reports put it, 'badly stung by the Bees' who handed out a 7-1 beating at Griffin Park.

Happily for football purposes, and by some design, Dickinson was soon back in home territory at HMS Collingwood in Fareham on radar, radio operating and plotter's courses and then subsequently at HMS Victory in Portsmouth itself.

His return to the area was marked by Pompey selecting him at inside-left for the home game in the War League South against Watford. Pompey lost 4-3 and long before the end, Dickinson had dropped back to his familiar left-half position. Any ideas that the club had about him repeating his youth club goalscoring feats as a professional lasted no more than an hour.

The first meeting and wartime presentation to the club president, then General Montgomery.

Continuous Naval football and the odd trophy as compensation.

Besides seeing out the rest of that season with Pompey, Dickinson was involved in a continuous round of Service football. After the first five games of the 1945-6 season, the inevitable overseas drafting interrupted his football career.

Jimmy Dickinson could never have been said to have been keen on life in the Forces but his general proficiency was such that he secured promotion and became Able-Bodied Seaman Dickinson. This was followed by a posting to one of the most modern and biggest destroyers to join the Fleet, HMS Carysfort which was part of the Sixth Destroyer Flotilla.

He was not to know, until they put to sea in September 1945, that he was headed for the East Indies Station (India, Ceylon, Singapore and Malta) and was to take part in the bombardments of the Indonesian Islands. Later, he ruefully recalled suffering the initiation ceremony traditionally practised on sailors as they crossed the Equator for the first time. In Dickinson's case it came in the Indian Ocean on 1 December 1945.

Every trip ashore coincided with a football match and Dickinson was kept busy running the ship's team. There were many strange games played during those months in the East Indies, on strange grounds and in strange climates. The return home meant dry land and the relative calm of the barracks at HMS Victory, close to the Portsmouth Naval Dockyard. Football for Pompey and base, command and naval representative teams saw Dickinson playing twice a week.

Every footballer and supporter waited for the return of League soccer with keen anticipation. After six years of war, people emerged gratefully, with a universal sigh of relief, as if from a long, dark tunnel. The return of the game would signal a return to normality, the offer of excitement and relaxation to a nation hungry for entertainment of any sort.

Boom years for the national game were just around the corner and for young Jimmy Dickinson there was a career and honours beyond his wildest dreams. He had already formed a fond attachment to Portsmouth Football Club and this was to grow into the love affair of a lifetime.

Opposite: The rising young star shows his paces as he takes up full-time training.

CHAMPIONSHIP DAYS

NEVER has the opening of a season been more keenly anticipated by players and supporters. The 1946-7 campaign — the first season of truly competitive football for seven years — heralded the start of a post-war boom in attendances at sporting fixtures. The public were desperate for entertainment and yearned to let their hair down. This was the dawn of a 'golden age' for the national game and there was plenty of young talent ready to make its mark. The only cloud on the horizon was the threat of a players' strike as they pressed for a £12 winter wage and £10 summer wage.

The excitement generated by soccer in those grim years is difficult to recapture in the 1980s. Even a pre-season trial, in which Dickinson scored a hat-trick, attracted a crowd of nearly 13,000. The interest was reflected in an average Fratton Park attendance of 30,000 for Pompey that season and even crowds of 8,000 for reserve games were not uncommon. It is amusing to recall from Mike Neasom's history of the club that the war shortages led to supporters answering appeals for 500 clothing coupons so that playing strips could be bought for the various Pompey sides.

Whilst football was a pleasant diversion from Dickinson's service duties, for the Portsmouth public it was a chance to seek relief from the harrowing scenes of war — the city was bombed quite badly — and the tension and stress of those recent times. The post-war economic conditions had led to overcrowding and congestion due to lack of living accommodation in Portsmouth and there was a strong desire for open spaces. Being crammed together on the packed terraces at Fratton Park might not quite have fulfilled that requirement but the genial company of one's fellow Pompey fans and the deeds of the heroes in blue shirts still made for light relief and an escape from the daily grind. For 90 minutes on a Saturday afternoon, nothing else mattered. Into this rarified atmosphere, football lifted its head once more.

Against this background young Jimmy Dickinson, still an amateur, was to mature as a half-back in this, Jack Tinn's last season as manager after 20 dramatic years. The biggest influence on the young wing-half was the veteran Scottish trainer-coach Jimmy Stewart, who was at pains to allow him to develop his own style and play his natural game.

The opening match of that 1946-7 season was also Dickinson's Football League debut and he played at right-

Above, top: Len Phillips and Dickinson into the Football League for the first time.

Above, bottom: The line-up for the start of the 1946-7 season: Back row (left to right): Wharton, Scoular, Rookes, Walker, Ferrier, Dickinson, Stewart (trainer), Phillips. Front: Barlow, Reid, Froggatt, McAlinden, Parker and Butler.

half in a 3-1 win over Blackburn Rovers at Fratton Park. Despite being two-footed, he started the season uneasily in that position. Pompey, too, found the going hard and by Christmas they were at the foot of the table. After eight matches 'out of position' Dickinson had been switched to his natural position of left-half in place of Guy Wharton to accommodate the tigerish Jimmy Scoular, acquired from Gosport whilst playing in Naval football. In October 1946, at Villa Park, the half-back line of Scoular, Flewin and Dickinson came together for the first time. It was a middle line which was to be the rock upon which the club's coming glories were founded.

As far as those early days are concerned, Jimmy Dickinson acknowledged later that having the experienced and stoic Reg Flewin alongside him at centre-half and the fine tactical skill of Harry Ferrier behind him at left-back made life easier. He was assured of an extended run in the first team in the absence of any real competition for the wing-half places, with the pre-war occupants of those positions, Guy Wharton and Jimmy Guthrie, by this time in the veteran stage.

Ready for the challenge of peacetime football, from left: Parker, Barlow, Scoular, McAlinden, Froggatt, Dickinson, Rookes, Ferrier, Flewin, Reid and Butler.

December 1946 at Blackburn Rovers and an anxious moment for Dickinson (left) and Flewin.

Pre-season cricket led by reserve team trainer Eddie Lever and Dickinson as the batsman.

The turning point of that first season came just after Christmas when a single goal victory at Blackburn coincided with the debut of inside-forward Len Phillips. Recruited from the Marines, Phillips was to be so influential in the coming seasons.

Results continued to improve as the season progressed and Pompey finished a respectable 12th in the First Division. AB Dickinson was still in the Royal Navy and, being stationed locally, he was in demand for Service football at all levels. He was an automatic choice for the Royal Navy in the Inter-Service tournaments and a match against the RAF at Villa Park saw him score a rare goal. The relationship between Pompey and the Navy was particularly good and, whenever possible, Dickinson would be released to play League soccer at weekends. In later years, as a club official, he would go out of his way to nurture Pompey's links with the local naval establishments.

The seeds of the Championship successes to come were sown that season with the introduction of players with whom the name of Jimmy Dickinson was to be irrevocably linked: Duggie Reid from Stockport, Jack Froggatt from the Royal Navy, Peter Harris from Gosport, Phil Rookes from Bradford *et al*. Every one of those players was a tribute to the talent-spotting skills of manager Jack Tinn during the war years.

It was a relaxed, happy season without any real pressure for success, an atmosphere reflected in the astonishing fact that only 12 players were sent off in the entire League programme. For Dickinson the only source of frustration was his continued National Service which prevented him signing full-time professional forms. Throughout that season he had held high hopes of his release. However, it seemed that every time the Prime Minister spoke publicly, Jimmy Dickinson's 'demob' day, along with that of thousands of others, seemed to drift that much further away.

Tinn's departure during the summer of 1947 was a surprise but the appointment of Bob Jackson, well known to the players as Pompey's chief scout, was well received and Dickinson was reassured by Jackson's great playing and coaching experience. The opening match of the 1947-8 campaign was marked by a home defeat by Burnley and Pompey's one effort of note was a rare shot by Dickinson which hit a post and bounced into the arms of goalkeeper Strong.

Dickinson's fine form for Pompey at the start of the season brought him to the attention of the game's more influential figures. Meanwhile, he was in constant midweek action in the United Services League, a local competition in which he played for the HMS Victory barracks side, where he was now permanently based in the centre of Portsmouth.

At last his patience was rewarded and, after nearly three years in the Navy, he was demobbed in October 1947. Portsmouth immediately signed the strapping 22-year-old — he stood 5ft 10in and weighed 12st 2lb — as a full-time professional but did not put him on the maximum weekly wage of £12 straight away. Within a few weeks came Jimmy Dickinson's first national recognition, albeit minor, with selection as reserve for a Football Association XI to meet the Army.

He soon began to feel the benefit of full-time training under Jimmy Stewart, although it would be true to say the team trained mostly by themselves. All Stewart was largely concerned about was keeping the players away from a football during the week — training in those days meant running and more running — and he made sure that Jimmy Dickinson received hardly any coaching. Stewart had a theory, which was difficult to disprove, that the less the players saw of the ball during training, the keener they would be to get hold of it on a Saturday afternoon. It was a philosophy also held by a trainer at Barnsley during Danny Blanchflower's days at Oakwell. Blanchflower used to counter by asking, "But when we get the ball, how will we know what to do with it?"

Back at Fratton Park, it was an inconsistent season for Pompey, whose most obvious problem was at centre-forward. Jackson bid for Tommy Lawton and was willing to pay £17,000 to Chelsea but the London club wanted to take Jimmy Dickinson in exchange and the proposed deal immediately foundered. The problem was solved by the astute signing of Ike Clarke, the powerfully-built West Bromwich Albion player, who Mike Neasom described in his history of the club as "the last link in the chain which was to carry Pompey to the pinnacle."

Portsmouth finished eighth, a position which did not reflect their continuing progress and the increasing maturity of Jimmy Dickinson's play. He appeared in all 42 matches and was the subject of several rave newspaper reports. Indeed, some football writers urged the England selectors to keep him in mind for the problem left-half position in the national team.

Pompey's team spirit thrived under the managership of the extrovert 'Bow-tie Bob', as Jackson was known to the players. The manager created a happy dressing-room atmosphere with his warm, thoughtful and sensitive approach which Dickinson, still a slightly shy, withdrawn young man, clearly appreciated. Not that this particular group of players demanded any great managerial skills from Jackson, whose greatest contribution had been as chief scout in previous years. He had introduced many of Pompey's current first-team squad to Fratton Park in the first place.

Dickinson epitomised the reliability and dedication within the team. Len Phillips recalled that there was never any call or need for team-talks as such. The manager, or the team for that matter, would not concern themselves with the merits of the opposition or any particular opposing player. If there was any outstanding player in the other side's ranks, such as Stanley Matthews or Tom Finney, the Pompey players would make contingency plans amongst themselves. They were highly self-motivated, knew what was expected of them on and off the pitch and there was certainly no need for the manager to have any concern for their corporate attitude.

Often, Dickinson and his colleagues would see the manager only for a minute or two in the dressing-room

Ready for training — Froggatt, Dickinson and Yeuell are with trainer Stewart.

Out on the town in Gothenburg during the 1948 Continental tour — from left: Froggatt, Ferrier, Dickinson, Rookes and Butler.

before kick-off, during which time his exhortations would be limited to a quick clap of the hands and an aside such as, "Come on lads, let's see if we can get another two points today, then." The team were an uncomplicated forthright collection of characters in those days, enjoying an average wage of £8 per week, reducing to £7 in the summer. Dickinson, like the others, carried his player's pass which, among other restrictions, provided that:

'Dancing is prohibited after Mondays'
'All players must be in the House not later than 10-30 p.m.'
'No player shall under any circumstances whatever own, use or travel in a motor-car'.

The latter restriction was originally imposed by Jack Tinn in the last season before the war, after wing-half Jimmy Guthrie had been involved in a serious motor accident on the morning before a game. The regulation was of sublime irony in view of the fact that the money which Portsmouth Football Club were paying Jimmy Dickinson would hardly have purchased a second-hand hulahoop.

By the approach of the club's golden jubilee season of 1948-9, the blend in the team looked right and, backed up by a driving confidence, they were eager to respond to the chairman's call to win the Championship. A superb start saw Pompey go 13 matches without defeat, during which Arsenal were the visitors on the club's golden jubilee day in November. The celebrations, led by Pompey's president Lord Montgomery, were climaxed by a 4-1 win over the Gunners and remained one of Jimmy Dickinson's happiest memories.

Pompey were well on their way to winning the First Division title for the first time in the club's history and over the season they were unbeaten at Fratton Park, winning 18 and drawing three of their 21 matches there. An attractive team to watch, they were also quite capable of 'looking after themselves' in any physical contest. The backbone was, of course, the half-back line where the rugged Scoular, later to win international honours for Scotland, Reg Flewin, the experienced quietly-spoken captain and centre-half, and Jimmy Dickinson, formed the rock upon which so many opposing attacks came to grief.

The individual styles of the two Jimmies were dissimilar but complemented each other, a blending of contrasts. Scoular was aggressive and powerful in the tackle — the late Duncan Edwards, something of an authority on the subject, rated him the finest tackler he ever saw — yet he was also a superb ball-player. Essentially an attacking wing-half, his main fault was that he could not suffer fools gladly on the field and, when a movement he had engineered was checked because of a team-mate's slow thinking, Scoular was sometimes prone to stay stranded and vexed in the wrong half of the field. That mattered less to Pompey because, some time before, Jimmy Dickinson would have slipped into position to cover the gap left by Scoular's excursion.

Unobtrusiveness, soundness and consistency — they

Above: Harris in action in the Golden Jubilee match against Arsenal. Opposite, centre: The young Jack Froggatt, tenacious outside-left.

Below: Clarke, Ferrier, Dickinson, Harris and Froggatt get in som

the ball.

The young Peter Harris, flying outside-right.

Action from the Golden Jubilee match against Arsenal – Froggatt (11) and Leslie Compton in an aerial duel watched by Dickinson (left), Clarke (9) and Joe Mercer (6).

The Championship trophy is there for all to see.

Mother and son get to work cleaning the trophies.

were the essentials of Dickinson's mainly defensive play in those halcyon days. After breaking up an opposition attack, he was usually content to slip the ball to the other Jimmy, who then launched Pompey's counter-attack. The understanding between these two players, so different in their skills, bordered on the telepathic. Jack Froggatt, the outside-left, also knew how much he owed to the faultless service from Jimmy Dickinson that season. Dickinson was now at his peak, with a polish and composure to his game which made him a certainty for an England cap sooner rather than later.

Massive support that season — the crowds dotted with the white caps of sailors — led to the record attendance of 51,385 squeezing into Fratton Park to see Derby County beaten 2-1 in the sixth round of the FA Cup. That victory put Portsmouth into the semi-final at Highbury. It was not to be Pompey's year, however, and against all the odds they went down 3-1 to Leicester City, then a lowly Second Division side. For much of the season there had been the prospect of Pompey becoming the first side in the 20th century to achieve the League and Cup 'double', although Dickinson later recalled that, unlike the media pressure of today, no one ever talked about winning the 'double' in those days. "With the League title virtually won, it was not the end of the world for us. The first priority was to win the Championship — something Pompey had never done. It was only later that we realised how near we had gone to making football history."

The players were complacent and ill-prepared for the semi-final. Like the 25,000 Pompey fans who travelled to London, they believed that the last hurdle before Wembley would be easily overcome. After the shock defeat rumours — perhaps inevitable, given the fans' acute disappointment — spread that there had been trouble in the Highbury dressing-room before the kick-off. It was alleged that the players were upset when they learned that Duggie Reid had not been selected, but Dickinson refuted the story. He added, "We did not lose merely by nerves or over-anxiousness, we had nearly all the play but Leicester deserved to win. It was a tactical defeat and we did not adapt to Leicester's breakaway game."

All this was put behind Pompey as they marched to the Championship, crushing Newcastle 5-0 at St James' Park and then hammering FA Cup Finalists, Wolves, by the same score. Pompey won the title without a single international player in their ranks and without spending big money in the transfer market. Without any obvious 'stars' and using only 18 players, the secret of their success lay simply in a great team spirit — the sort of spirit that Dickinson was to miss so desperately at times later in his career. Deeply enthusiastic, with great commitment, the 'Iron Men of Portsmouth', as they were known, never knew when they were beaten. As Dickinson once reflected, "If we were a goal down, even two, nobody worried. We just got on with the job, fought back and usually won."

He remembered the grudging respect from the newspapers, although it is strange to recall that Pompey's play attracted some criticism from the nationals. "Too robust and tackling inclined to be clumsy," was a typical

Dickinson and Froggatt see the ball safely back to Butler in goal as Stoke City threaten – November 1951.

comment. While their strength lay in a defence which conceded only 42 goals — with goalkeeper Ernie Butler consistently reliable — the system, devised by the players, where Ike Clarke played slightly behind the forwards was hugely successful. Each of the aggressive, fast-moving forward line reached double figures in the scoring charts. Rumbustious, flaxen-haired 'Jolly Jack' Froggatt and the flying Peter Harris were on the wings, the rangy Duggie Reid and Clarke were the central strikers and the skilful Len Phillips acted as provider.

Jimmy Dickinson typified the spirit in the team. Late in the season Pompey were involved in a vital match at Bolton and Dickinson ignored the advice of the club doctor not to play because of a cut forehead sustained on Easter Monday at Birmingham. The stitches were removed before the match at Burnden Park and the wound reopened after ten minutes. Carrying a cloth to stem the blood and unable to head the ball, Dickinson somehow got through the second-half, helping Pompey to the two points which clinched the title.

The players' bonus for winning the Championship was £550 talent money from the League, to be shared by the team, and the club also presented each man with a £10 voucher which could be spent in any Portsmouth shop.

For Jimmy Dickinson and Peter Harris, however, there was a reward which they undoubtedly valued far higher than money and the Pompey pair were selected for the England party to visit Scandinavia that summer. Alas, almost immediately, Harris was forced to withdraw through injury, leaving Dickinson to make his debut for the England 'B' team in Finland, followed by rapid promotion to the senior side for the full international in Norway.

With their first Championship secured, Pompey went on to revive the fashion of winning the title two years in succession. It was a feat which had not been achieved for 15 years, not since Arsenal's hat-trick of League Championships in the 1930s, although seven of those intervening seasons had been suspended because of war. There was only one major change in the Portsmouth line-up for this second title-winning season. Bill Hindmarsh replaced Phil Rookes at full-back and the team-spirit was

reinforced by a successful close-season tour of Sweden and Denmark which Dickinson was pleased to join late after his England travels.

The Pompey team again played to the ceiling of their ability and, despite his almost continuous diet of football since the war, Jimmy Dickinson showed no signs of staleness. By now he was an established star, by virtue of his outstanding international debut, and very much a favourite of the Press. The same could not be said of the team, however, and like any successful and all-powerful combination they attracted their share of criticism.

Competition was stiffer that season but Pompey gave notice of their challenge early on when they won 5-1 at Middlesbrough. Dickinson gave one of his finest attacking displays, functioning as a forward for much of the match and supplying several defence-splitting passes. His new and influential role was again seen to good effect in the 7-0 thrashing of Everton at Fratton Park and local journalists were in no doubt about the stature of 'the debonair prince of half-backs' as one writer christened him.

The Championship was finally achieved by a well-timed and storming finish to the season with 17 points coming from the last 11 games. The final match still had to be won, however, and in an electric atmosphere Bill Thompson, normally a reserve half-back, scored only 20 seconds from the kick-off against Aston Villa. Everybody was aware that Wolves could take the title if Pompey slipped but Thompson added another and Reid netted a hat-trick to sink Villa 5-1. It was enough to give Portsmouth the title which was decided on goal-average for the first time since 1924. At the end of the day, Pompey were two-fifths of a goal better off than Wolves.

Dickinson still lived at Alton and made the daily trip to Portsmouth by train. In the close season, however, he bought his first motor-car and secured permission from the directors to become the first Pompey footballer since the war to own and drive a vehicle. Most of his playing colleagues lived within a couple of miles of the ground and the local 'bus services met their travel needs.

As if all the tension of the title race that season was not enough, Dickinson soon found himself en route to South America with the England party, bound for the 'glamour' of Rio de Janeiro and a disastrous World Cup campaign.

The post-war soccer boom was inevitably showing signs of decline by the opening of the 1950-51 season and Jimmy Dickinson and, more particularly, Pompey found the going much harder as opponents looked to match the League Champions physically. Dickinson was clearly not at his best that season and even his enthusiasm was dulled after months of continuous football, including the long trip to Brazil for the World Cup. Until his demob he had been at the beck and call of the Royal Navy; now he was in constant demand as the Football League and the Football Association arranged the round of representative matches.

Jimmy Dickinson in training.

Today, clubs are more protective towards their players but in the 1950s they were expected to release them for all manner of matches. These games were usually played in midweek and in addition to the inter-League affairs, Dickinson seemed to be selected for just about everything — including a London Combination XI to play in Paris, even though he had never played in a Combination game. Over a two-year period he usually played in two games a week and it was small wonder that his life revolved around football and left little time for outside interests other than the occasional game of tennis or golf. Certainly there was little opportunity for the young man to have any sort of social life or meet a nice young Alton girl — as Jimmy's mother would remind him.

Pompey were continually dogged by injuries and sickness that season, with six or seven reserves playing in the first team at any one time, and the campaign turned out to be an anti-climax after the high excitement of the title wins. In truth, the enthusiasm necessary to complete a hat-trick of Championship successes was never there and the battle-cry of the famous old 'Chimes' was seldom heard from the terraces.

Jimmy Dickinson was now paid the maximum weekly wage of £12 and had qualified for a benefit £750 although, after income tax had been deducted, only £400 found its way into his bank account. For Portsmouth, his only other moment of note that season was his first goal in four years' of League football when he scored with a 40-yard free-kick against Charlton Athletic at Fratton Park. A rare goal from Jimmy Scoular in the same match earned Pompey a thrilling 3-3 draw. From that moment on, matches against Charlton seemed to feature largely in Dickinson's career and the Haddicks became favourite adversaries.

Halfway through the season, Reg Flewin's injury threatened to disrupt Pompey's defence but the situation was retrieved by the astute switch of Jack Froggatt to centre-half. Dickinson needed to adjust to a more defensive role, typical of his early playing days, with Froggatt an unorthodox, mobile defender and by no means the 'stopper' type. It was a partnership which was to be extended to international level, although not immediately. When Froggatt was given his full England debut in the Wembley showpiece against Scotland in April 1951, Dickinson was curiously overlooked for the prestigious fixture.

That summer brought Jimmy Dickinson an introduction to a young lady on her first visit to England, for a six-month holiday from Singapore with her parents. Catherine Ann Quinton was working at Blake Maternity Home in Gosport as part of her nursing and midwifery training. It was a tennis match at the Seacourt Club on Hayling Island, involving some Pompey players, that saw the first meeting between the trainee nurse and the shy 26-year-old international footballer from Alton. Despite having absolutely no interest in football, Ann was sufficiently 'smitten' to accept Jimmy's invitations to forthcoming matches. His first serious relationship, extended when Ann moved to Alton General Hospital towards the end of her

Opposite: Ike Clarke gets ready to shoot at the Villa goal while Bert Barlow (in front of referee) watches.

Below: Harris gets in his cross against Chelsea at Stamford Bridge despite the attention of a young Ron Greenwood.

stay, was to lead to their marriage almost four years later. In between, Ann left England for Malaya to nurse tuberculosis patients before returning to Alton General and a permanent position in 1955, followed by their marriage.

Portsmouth's playing fortunes were on the decline as the Championship-winning players began to age and the club failed to sign adequate replacements at this most critical time. The greatest highlight of Pompey's season was their progress in the FA Cup. They reached the quarter-finals before losing 4-2 in an epic tie against Newcastle United at Fratton Park.

Emphatic victories in earlier rounds against lesser opposition — Lincoln City, Notts County and Doncaster Rovers — had given rise to hopes of a Wembley Final appearance that year. In the event, the Newcastle encounter was said to be 'the greatest Final Wembley had never seen'. As far as Jimmy Dickinson was concerned, there was no doubt that, from the first whistle to the last, it was the most pulsating, exciting match of his career, despite the result.

Newcastle were looking to win the Cup for the second year in succession and the Fratton tie was clearly their biggest hurdle so far. Geoffrey Green of *The Times* was moved to rate the match as one of the best three club matches he had seen in 30 years of reporting soccer. His romantic report read, in part, 'One would have wished that all the sceptics of this world could have been at Fratton

Park on Saturday. Here was a grey afternoon touched by glory. As the battle swayed back and forth, those of us compressed around its fiery edges became a part of it, so that at the end we were left in a strange state of nervous exhaustion and exhilaration.'

Pompey took the lead after only four minutes but then Dickinson and centre-half Froggatt were stretched to the limit by the Newcastle attack. The Magpies' front line, inspired by the great Jackie Milburn, gave an awesome display of shooting power. Milburn played Pompey

Pompey pictured with the League Championship trophy and the FA Charity Shield in 1949. Back row (left to right): Bob Jackson (m (trainer). Front: Harris, Delaphena, Clarke, Ferrier, Stephen, Phillips, Froggatt. Jimmy Dickinson apparently missed the photo call.

virtually on his own and it often took two men to cover and tackle him as he showed all his uncanny control and pace. His three goals won the match for Newcastle and his third goal was one of the finest ever seen at Fratton Park — an oblique shot from just outside the penalty-

area into the far top corner of the net. There were 15 minutes left and up to that point the match had been finely balanced at 2-2. Pompey, driven on by Dickinson's tireless efforts, had enjoyed the slight edge but Milburn turned the course of the game and a fourth goal, from Robledo in the last minute, made doubly sure. It was a crushing blow and never again in Jimmy Dickinson's lifetime were Pompey to come so close to Wembley.

Morale was low and before the season was out, Arsenal tried to capitalise on this by making a joint offer for Dickinson and Jack Froggatt. Clearly there was never any question of manager Jackson allowing Dickinson to move and a similar public uproar prevented him considering the release of Froggatt.

Despite Pompey's moderate playing record, the international recognition which the team earned that season was unprecedented. It was a proud and unique day for the club when the entire half-back line — Scoular for Scotland, Froggatt and Dickinson for England — played in the last Home International Championship game of 1951-2.

By the end of that season, Jimmy Dickinson was exhausted. Since the war he had played football almost continually and his League appearances for Pompey read: 40 games in 1946-7; 42 in 1947-8; 41 in 1948-9; 40 in 1949-50; and 41 in 1950-51. There were also 14 FA Cup ties, not to mention international, inter-League, representative and service commitments. Yet he had maintained a consistently high level of performance and retained his England place through all the peaks and troughs at club level and despite not being associated with a 'fashionable' London club.

He departed for the England summer tour to Europe — a trip which was to include a famous victory in Vienna — oblivious to the fact that a change of manager at Fratton Park was to be announced. It was a change which was to herald a new era for Pompey and, for Jimmy, the renewal of an association which began in his schooldays 20 years earlier.

ular, Thompson, Reid, Butler, Rookes, Hindmarsh, Yeuell, Stewart

Duggie Reid (centre) outjumps everyone to score against Manchester United. Peter Harris is fourth from left, Tommy Brown is wearing number eight.

35

CAPTAINCY
WITH LEVER

Above: The proud young man with his first motor-car.

Opposite: Football League representative honours, September 1952. Back row: Lofthouse, Garrett, the trainer, Merrick, Dickinson, Froggatt. Front: Finney, Sewell, Wright, Ramsey, Baily, Elliott. Nat Lofthouse scored six of the League's goals as they hammered the Irish League 7-1 at Molineux.

EDDIE Lever's emergence from the shadows, after his years since the war as Reserve-team manager, greeted Jimmy Dickinson upon his return from England's tour. Lever's appointment as manager to replace Bob Jackson, who had accepted a lucrative offer to move to Hull City, obviously delighted Dickinson and the promotion of his mentor cemented an already close relationship between the two men. It also brought the player even closer to his club.

Early in 1952-3, Dickinson achieved his second appearance milestone when he became the first Pompey footballer to play in 250 League games for the club. Earlier he had beaten Cliff Parker's record of 244 appearances.

Almost immediately Lever took over as manager he found his relationship with Jimmy Scoular was an unhappy one and throughout the season the fiery Scot sought a transfer as a result of tempting approaches from Newcastle United. Scoular's departure at the end of the season broke up the Championship-winning half-back line and signalled the start of Pompey's defensive problems which, despite Dickinson's efforts, were not to be solved in the coming years.

Less significantly, the directors announced that players were now permitted to own or travel in motor-cars. In

An evening of snooker for Eddie Lever and his team.

The three friends in practice– Peter Harris, Duggie Reid and Dickinson.

From left: Harris, Mansell, Barnard, Dickinson, Reid, Gordon and Henderson talk tactics.

reality the rule had not been enforced for some years and Dickinson had driven into work every day. The board's new latitude even extended to dancing which was now permitted on a Tuesday evening, whereas previously the rule was 'no dancing after Monday'. Again this was of no real concern to Dickinson, for he was never one to be spotted in any of the Portsmouth clubs or ballrooms anyway.

He missed only one match that season, when he and Froggatt played in the Saturday afternoon international against Scotland. Reg Pickett, his deputy who had waited so long in the wings, took his rare opportunity well and Pompey beat Newcastle 5-1 without their star players. Pompey finished a disappointing 15th in Division One and the club's perennial problem at centre-forward was only partially resolved by the late signing of 31-year-old former England 'B' international Charlie Vaughan from Charlton. In truth, Dickinson did not have a good season by his own high standards, despite retaining his England place, and the local *Football Mail* even levelled some criticism at the Fratton favourite, "In recent matches Dickinson has neutralised some good work by giving the ball straight to the opposition."

As the 1953-4 season opened, Pompey were clearly in need of some inspiration and, despite his 'moderate' form at club level in the previous campaign, it was inevitable that Dickinson would be Lever's choice as the new captain. Dickinson's main task was to knit the team together in an attempt to improve on the indifferent form of the previous term. He took over the leadership at a difficult time, when Pompey urgently needed to replace some of their ageing stars. The team spent the season in a constant state of reorganisation and there was a high level of inexperience within the ranks.

It was a difficult season for Jimmy Dickinson and a sign of times to come as he played himself to a standstill in every match, helping to cover in defence and trying to start up attacks wherever possible. Lever, now desperate to steady the defence, installed the veteran Duggie Reid at centre-half alongside Dickinson and new young full-backs Jack Mansell and Alex Wilson had been introduced. Attendances at Fratton Park had fallen from the halcyon days and crowds now numbered less than 30,000, which might seem high by today's standards but which gave cause for concern in 1954 when they were amongst the worst attendance figures in Division One.

The main drama was again reserved for the FA Cup, although once more there was ultimate disappointment. In January 1954, Pompey drew their third-round tie at home to Charlton, 3-3 after being 3-1 down in the second half. The midweek replay at The Valley saw the return of Flewin at centre-half. It was his first FA Cup-tie for three years and Pompey won a thrilling match in extra-time. When Harris scored what proved to be the winning goal, it was the first time that Pompey had taken the lead in the two games. Charlton, having been ahead four times in all, were beaten at the death. Dickinson looked back on that replay as one of his finest club performances. 'Nimrod' in the *Football Mail* reported that in defence

Dickinson's tackles had a 'speedy ferocity about them' and in attack he produced 'the best shot I have ever seen him deliver, brilliantly saved by Bartram'.

The fourth round produced a marathon three games in ten days against Scunthorpe United of the Third Division North before Pompey won the tie on neutral ground at Highbury. These were hard, physical battles for Dickinson and his fellow defenders on heavy, snow-covered pitches. The players were also conscious of the inexperience of amateur goalkeeper Mervyn Gill, an RAF serviceman brought in to replace the injured Ted Platt.

A goalless fifth-round match at Bolton brought great hope of further advancement and this was evidenced by the hundreds of supporters waiting to meet the players at the railway station on their return. Excitement mounted in the town and for the first time since 1949, the gates were locked at Fratton Park as nearly 46,000 saw Pompey lose the replay 2-1. They never recovered from conceding a goal in the first minute but superb wing-half play by Dickinson and Len Phillips, now settled in that position after his conversion from inside-forward, was a positive feature of the unsuccessful struggle.

Almost immediately another link with Jimmy Dickinson's past was broken when Jack Froggatt's unsettled spell at the club was ended by his transfer to

Above: The two captains, Peter Goring of Arsenal and Dickinson of Pompey, shake hands.
Below: Meeting as opponents for the first time. Dickinson greets his old club and international colleague Jack Froggatt, back as captain of Leicester City.

The local newspaper's cartoonist 'Plum' pays tribute.

Leicester City. With the subsequent departure of Harry Ferrier, Dickinson was left with only his dear friends Harris, Phillips and Reid as fellow survivors from the Championship days. By the end of that season Dickinson had stretched his League appearances to 324 and, although there was never any doubt about his supreme fitness and stamina, it would have been difficult at that stage to envisage him going on to more than double that figure, given his demanding role.

Inevitably, his extraordinary luck with injury altered as the 1954-5 season dawned and he found himself on the sidelines for the first six matches after sustaining a niggling ankle injury in pre-season training. It gave another chance for Pickett, who was thirsty for an extended run in the team and who, after five years as an eternal reserve, must have thought that such a chance would never come.

No sooner had Dickinson returned to the team and contributed to Pompey's fine start to the season than he broke his left ankle against Cardiff City. He stumbled over an opponent in the first half and played on with the ankle strapped. With 13 minutes to go, Eddie Lever called him off the field and not before time. It was not Dickinson's happiest memory — "It was certainly the most painful one, especially that first night in hospital," he said later. The ankle went into plaster and Dickinson spent a very frustrating three and a half months waiting through the slow mending process. One compensation was that it gave him more opportunity to see Ann Quinton in her lodgings at Alton General Hospital where she had returned after her spell abroad. It was, of course, no coincidence that Ann had secured a place in Alton to practise her midwifery. Dickinson was also able to spend some time with Alton Football Club, helping with their preparations and tactics during their coincidental good run in the FA Amateur Cup.

In February 1955, when Jimmy Dickinson tested the carefully-bandaged ankle in a midweek reserve fixture, after 12 weeks' absence, the statisticians were quick to point out that it was the first time that he had played in a club team outside the First Division in his eight years as a professional. His eventual return to the first team coincided with the loss of Len Phillips with a knee injury, ironically incurred while with the England party in a practice match against Charlton Athletic behind 'closed doors' at The Valley. It was a particularly savage blow for the player, his club and country because Phillips was then at the peak of his mercurial skills. It was also an injury which required months of recuperation and which ended in such bitter disappointment when Phillips broke down in his comeback match.

Despite these injuries, there was a happy club spirit with the experienced players working closely with Eddie Lever on tactics and systems. Many a match strategy was formulated during long train journeys to away games. That great tactician, Duggie Reid, would expound his theories in the restaurant car with the aid of salt, mustard and vinegar pots, forks, spoons and cubes of sugar all representing the players. 'Nimrod' of the *Football Mail* remembered once that the players were so engrossed that

Above: The shy member of a distinguished sports panel – from left: Chris Chataway, athlete, Rex Alston, commentator, Dickinson and Roger Bannister, athlete.
Opposite: Another meeting of the captain and the club's famous president, Field Marshall Viscount Montgomery of Alamein.
Below: Captain and centre-half for the 1956-7 season. Back: Wilson, J. Phillips, Uprichard, Albury, Weddle and Mansell. Front: Harris, Gordon, Dickinson, McClellan and Henderson.

they failed to see the dining-car steward clearing the tables. It was only when the sugar cubes were whisked back into their bowl that anything amiss was noticed. Duggie Reid was apparently heard to remark, "He's mucked up the sweetest formation you ever saw."

Chelsea won the Championship that season and Pompey secured third place, tucking in behind runners-up Wolves on goal-average and edging ahead of Sunderland — who also had the same number of points — by virtue of the second goal scored towards the end of a 5-2 defeat at Bramall Lane in the last match of the season. That high placing was to be the last major achievement by the Portsmouth side of the post-war years and Dickinson was not to know that from that point on, Pompey would slide towards inevitable relegation in three years and decline even further into the lower divisions.

The close season brought the usual matches for England, this time in Spain and Portugal, before Jimmy Dickinson returned for his marriage to Ann in June 1955, in the village church at Chawton, with Reg Flewin as his best man. After a West Country honeymoon the couple set up home in Alton, in a house in which Ann still lives. It was a marriage of opposites: Ann, forthright but charming with no interest in football; Jimmy, quiet and homely but completely immersed in the game. Ann recalls that her husband would generally get his own way, even though she was, by her own admission, the dominant partner. Home was a refuge for Jimmy Dickinson, a haven way out of reach of Portsmouth, where he could settle down with his pipe and pick up the *Daily Telegraph* crossword or a book of the 'thriller' type. Ann's first major challenges were getting him used to doing some of the domestic chores, which he had been used to leaving to his mother, and introducing him to the delights of Malaysian cooking.

The 1955-6 season was notable for the departure from the playing scene of Dickinson's good friend Duggie Reid, who took up the occupancy and control of a hostel for the club's youth players. The dour Scot maintained his close association with both Jimmy Dickinson and the Pompey club and later became groundsman at Fratton Park, a job he retained until his recent retirement. That season saw Pompey stage the first floodlit Football League match. It was against Newcastle United in February 1956 and, with his dry humour, Dickinson was particularly amused when the lights failed half-an-hour before the start and the players were forced to change in dressing-rooms lit by one small hurricane-lamp and dozens of candles. Supporters waited outside in long queues before the fuse was mended and the match started ten minutes late.

Pompey slipped to 12th place that season and there was concern for the future. The Championship-winning side was now represented only by Dickinson and Peter Harris and there was no money available from the directors to buy quality players. It transpired that this was to be the first of many difficult campaigns which Jimmy Dickinson was to experience in the years to come. Eddie Lever was a popular and considerate manager but he lacked the hard, driving approach and some luck, both of which

were needed to rally a dispirited team.

The writing was now on the wall. Pompey won only one of their first ten matches and an injury to Phil Gunter, their young centre-half, compounded the crisis. Dickinson immediately agreed to Eddie Lever's appeal for him to switch to centre-half, a move which was the only logical option since Pompey's rearguard desperately needed the England man's vast experience. Bill Albury, a promising local discovery, was ready to take over at left-half and Dickinson knew that such a switch would almost certainly signal the end of his international career, already under threat from the prodigious Duncan Edwards. He said, "I have been told that if I move from left-half, the selectors will not consider me for England." Yet he never hesitated to meet Pompey's need and his first match in the number-five shirt, at Arsenal, typified his commitment. Portsmouth drew 1-1 at Highbury and Dickinson was hoarse at the end after urging on his colleagues in one of his stirring and vociferous performances.

For the rest of that season Jimmy Dickinson was to cover a tremendous amount of ground from his new role, attempting to bolster weaknesses elsewhere. He would gain

Jimmy Dickinson and his bride, Ann, after their wedding at Chawton.

Derek Dougan at 19, Lever's last signing.

Crawford was soon injured and the extrovert, flamboyant skills of Dougan were introduced. Dickinson found the strong-minded Dougan's antics not always to his taste, but even he marvelled at the Irishman's first League goal when it came against Wolves. Dougan first teased Dickinson's close friend Billy Wright and then slipped the ball through the England captain's legs before racing 25 yards to shoot past Bert Williams. It brought the Fratton Park crowd to their feet.

Lever's position as manager became even more untenable as the team showed no sign of improvement, despite Dickinson's increasing contributions off the field, and there was a suspicion locally that the directors were having an increasing say in team selection. Yet again Dickinson appeared in every match and, incredibly,

Heading duel between Dickinson and Foulkes of Newcastle United.

relegation was again avoided. This time Pompey escaped only on goal-average and they could look back on a 3-3 home draw with Manchester United, late in the season, as the turning point. Two goals behind at half-time, Pompey fought back to win a crucial point.

Ironically, for most of that season Dickinson was back to left-half with Cyril Rutter at centre-half. By now, though, his England place had been irretrievably lost, despite the tragic death of his successor, Duncan Edwards, in the Munich air disaster.

Within days of the season ending came the news that Eddie Lever had been dismissed. Despite the inevitability of the situation, Jimmy Dickinson was sad and upset at the sacking of his dear friend and the end of Lever's 30-year association with Portsmouth Football Club. Footballers usually adapt quickly to the demise of one manager and the installation of another, but Pompey's players were genuinely sorry to see Lever go. They were to be even more dismayed after the appointment of his successor.

Like the ending of any love affair, the parting was painful and bitter. Eddie Lever returned to teaching in the locality and eventually became a headmaster. He broke with football irrevocably and never again set foot inside Fratton Park.

even more admiration from the Fratton faithful for his immaculate centre-half play which showed uncanny anticipation. Yet even he could do nothing to prevent some crushing defeats, of which the most painful was a 6-0 humiliation at Wolverhampton on his 400th League appearance. A temporary switch back to wing-half to help counter the skills of Tom Finney at Deepdale was singularly unsuccessful and his former England colleague had a field day with a hat-trick in Preston's 7-1 win.

Relegation was narrowly avoided on the strength of three successive wins, with no goals conceded, over the Easter period. After doing the 'double' over Cardiff City and beating Wolves at Fratton, Pompey were safe. Jimmy Dickinson, an ever-present that season, had made an immense contribution to Portsmouth's salvation and he was overjoyed — "It feels just like it did when we won the Championship."

Dickinson reconciled himself to another season of struggle, with no new additions to the playing strength, but Lever quickly recruited Derek Dougan, a 19-year-old centre-forward from Belfast. With the emergence of young Ray Crawford, there was the promise of more goals but

TROUBLE AND STRIFE WITH COX

IF Dickinson was upset over Eddie Lever's dismissal, it would be true to say that he was also uneasy about the appointment of former Arsenal winger Freddie Cox as Lever's successor. Dickinson was singularly unimpressed with Cox's qualifications. During his time as manager of Third Division Bournemouth, Cox had antagonised many people and surprised the Cherries' supporters with his revolutionary methods. Certainly he had never been afraid to express his opinions forcefully.

Cox's reputation had been gained the previous season, solely on the strength of three FA Cup matches against First Division opposition. Bournemouth had knocked out Wolves at Molineux, then defeated Spurs at Dean Court before falling unluckily to Manchester United in the quarter-finals. Their performances were riddled with gimmicks dreamed up by Cox — a deep-lying centre-forward, forwards with different numbers on their backs, obstructions at throw-ins and so on. The latter tactic provoked much interest when Ollie Norris was detailed to jump up and down in front of the opposing thrower. Nevertheless, Bournemouth's success tempted the Portsmouth directors to offer Cox the challenge of saving their ailing club's First Division status for the 1958-9 season. Ultimately the appointment was an unmitigated disaster

and Dickinson would never forgive the Board for their choice. In fairness to Cox, the Portsmouth club was already in decline and the seeds of his failures had already been sown.

Pre-season interest in the new manager and his seven signings — who had largely been gathered cheaply from the lower divisions — was great, but turmoil was already breaking out within the Fratton corridors. Dickinson and the other established stars found it difficult to accept Cox's fresh ideas and, more particularly, the 'army style' training routines. A stream of petty rules and regulations were imposed on established and junior players alike and, in handling his men, Cox was a martinet, convinced that discipline and minute attention to detail was the way to win. Such methods have proved successful many times in the modern game, but not when the manager fails to win the respect of the players or to secure the affection in which his predecessor had been held.

As far as the senior players were concerned, their relationship with Cox soon deteriorated into mutual antipathy. Cox found it impossible to overcome the immediate resentment Dickinson and Peter Harris, for instance, felt at his replacing Eddie Lever. Furthermore, he did not endear himself to those two by his continual references to the attributes of his former club, Arsenal, and by wearing the Gunners' blazer. It all added up to what Dickinson described as "the most disappointing season I have had since I began my career."

A 'plan' devised by Cox and worked on by the players in the pre-season period was misunderstood by them and it was discarded at the 11th hour, just before the first match of the season. When it was reintroduced after the early disastrous weeks, it still took the players some time to get the hang of it. With hindsight, the plan was clearly ahead of its time, but it was dubbed a 'Third Division idea' by the supporters. The strategy was to bring wingers back in deep-lying left and right-half positions whenever the team lost possession, then revert to the normal wing positions when the ball was regained. In the end, the system fell down because of the players' inability and Cox's persistence with it when it was not working. Despite Dickinson's feelings about the tactics, only privately expressed, the results might have been more striking if Cox had been able to use the system with the right set

Opposite: A welcome dip. From left: Carter, Harris, John Phillips, Gunter, McGhee, Hayward and Dickinson.

Below: Freddie Cox – some initial unease over his appointment.

of players. Even when the opposition were confused, the Pompey players were unable to capitalise on it.

Dickinson began the season at centre-half but, by November, had reverted to wing-half to replace the ineffectual Tommy Casey, an expensive signing from Newcastle. Basil Hayward, the new centre-half, found difficulty in bridging the gap between First Division soccer and Third Division football with Port Vale. Acute defensive problems were reflected in a pathetic run from 22 November 1958 to the end of the season. Twenty defeats in 24 matches in that period committed Pompey to relegation and the 21-points return for the whole season marked the depths to which performances and discord within the club had sunk.

Small matters became crises and niggling worries were magnified. The players were irritated by petty restrictions such as being forbidden to drive to the ground and being told to walk instead. On Friday evenings the assistant trainers were to be found calling at players' digs to ensure that they were tucked up in bed and not out socialising in the town.

Derek Dougan, that astute signing by Lever, found himself in direct conflict with Cox, particularly over Dougan's extravagant antics on the pitch, and the player was eventually sold to Blackburn Rovers. Before his departure, Dougan was disappointed that the senior professionals — and he included Dickinson in this — did not convey the players' feelings to the directors. He later recalled that when the chairman called a dressing-room inquest into the club's problems, no one spoke up and 'a player who had won nearly 50 caps was looking at the ground throughout.'

Dickinson's 500th League appearance came at White Hart Lane and it summed up the season. After leading 3-1, Pompey had to settle for a draw after a doubtful penalty and an equaliser had been conceded in the last few minutes. After a calamitous 5-3 home defeat by Wolves on Boxing Day 1958, Dickinson was 'rested' for the return at Molineux the next day. Not only did it mean that, unusually, Dickinson was able to spend the whole Christmas period at home that year, it was also the first time that he had missed a first-team match other than due to injury or international calls. In his absence the defence was routed 7-0 — Pompey's sixth defeat in succession — and he was instantly recalled.

Dickinson was hurt and disappointed as Pompey slipped to the bottom of the First Division and stared relegation in the face as early as the turn of the year. How exasperated he was as, match after match, mistakes lost them precious points. Yet never once did Dickinson show his displeasure and it was never his way to shout reproofs at colleagues on the field. The only hint would be a slight shake of the head as he strode purposefully back into position, then at once it was back to the game. Few could have felt the sadness of Pompey's decline that season as keenly as Jimmy Dickinson. He remembered, "It was worse than going down to the Third Division two years later because it was the first time the club had been relegated in our history."

By his own admission, the slump in Pompey's fortunes contributed to his continuing as a player rather than, as might have been expected, hastening his retirement. Dickinson might well have been content to hang up his boots if Portsmouth had remained an established First Division side with a talented crop of players pressing for his place. As it was, not for the first time, his deep sense of loyalty made it impossible for him to desert the club.

With relegation assured, Cox 'rested' Dickinson again — neither the club or the media could bring themselves to refer to his being 'dropped' — for the final home match. The local *Evening News* commented, "It looks like the beginning of the end of Dickinson for whom the club plan a gradual run-down until he takes up a coaching appointment." They were not to know that he was to prolong his 'run-down' to retirement for another six years!

Dickinson was recalled, on sentimental grounds, for the last First Division match of the season and, as it transpired, the last of his career. At Highbury he captained the team from right-half in a 5-2 defeat. Dickinson had netted few goals in his career but he marked the occasion by scoring the best — a calmly-placed left-foot shot from 20 yards after combining with Peter Harris. Portsmouth were thus relegated after 32 years of First Division football. Only goalscorer Ron Saunders and battling Harry Harris offered real hopes for a better future.

At the age of 34, Jimmy Dickinson was destined to play outside the First Division for the first time. Lord Montgomery of Alamein, never a man to take a passive role as Club President, wrote to Sir Stanley Rous, President of FIFA, demanding to know what corrective action should be taken. Should the manager go? And, wonderful player and pleasant man though he was, had Dickinson the leadership qualities to remain as captain? Defeat does not just happen, someone had failed — that was Monty's theme. Rous's reply is not documented.

The close season found Dickinson still resisting the appeals from his sisters to finish with football and retire to the pleasures of running a small shop or business in or around Alton. The love of playing the game itself was still so strong, almost addictive by now.

Pompey's fall into the Second Division brought no respite from the anguish of poor results. Cox sought to solve one of the many defensive problems by switching Dickinson to the new position, for him, of left-back. Basil Hayward returned to the centre-half position after a stormy first-team passage in that position the previous season. Even during the first weeks of the 1959-60 campaign, the situation looked desperate. With no financial resources, the club were forced into an all-out dependence on young players who were not given the time they so vitally needed to raise their game to Second Division standard.

Dickinson was captaining a side devoid of confidence, spirit and talent. Indeed, no captain could have had a more trying time. That period tested his unique loyalty to the full but his philosphical, placid nature saw him through. Curiously, the young wing-half, Ron Howells, was nominated by Cox as the next team captain to replace Dickinson, who was given the job of grooming the

The relegated eleven. Back (left to right): Gunter, J. Phillips, Uprichard, Hayward, Dickinson and Casey. Front: P. Harris, Gordon, Saunders, H. Harris and Newman. Below: Dickinson and Newcastle's White in a heading duel during Pompey's relegation season.

youngster for the post in anticipation of his own move to a coaching job. Dickinson's reaction to these plans for his future is not recorded, but the local *Football Mail* was in no mood to hasten Dickinson's departure from the scene. It commented, 'He will decide for himself when the time has come.'

The playing crisis deepened and was summed up, first by a 6-3 defeat at the hands of Huddersfield in October — after Pompey had been three goals ahead — and by a calamitous FA Cup defeat at home by Fourth Division newcomers Peterborough United. The latter was a particularly painful memory for Dickinson because Hails, the Posh outside-right, led him a merry dance and finally beat him for speed to score the last-minute winner. The defeat brought the first 'secret' round-the-table discussion to find the causes of the club's ills and Dickinson represented the players at the meeting with the manager, chairman and vice-chairman. Naturally he felt inhibited and then, as always, there was never any question of him 'rocking the boat'. Whether by coincidence or otherwise, the club's next act was to secure a new club captain with the purchase of centre-half Brian Snowden from Blackpool. Dickinson was clearly relieved to step down and was finding the going hard. He said, "Division Two football is harder if anything — less skilful, but harder."

The distance and feeling between the older players and Cox was highlighted that autumn when Peter Harris

requested a transfer. Club loyalist Harris, then 33 years old, was totally disillusioned by the authoritarian regime. Southampton were showing interest in securing his services when he and his legion of fans were stunned by the outcome of a routine medical check-up at the club. A serious chest ailment was diagnosed and Dickinson's close friend and the last playing link with the Championship days spent almost five months in a sanatorium in the Hampshire countryside, close enough for Dickinson to visit him regularly. Harris recovered but it signalled the end of the golden days for the speedy winger, after 479 League appearances and a record 194 goals.

Harry Harris, a real hope for Pompey's future.

Just before Christmas, Pompey enjoyed their first home League win for 11 months and that gave rise to hopes of a revival. There was a desperate scramble to escape relegation and safety was secured by a margin of three points, although the issue was not settled until the last match. A happy aspect was the Phil Gunter-Dickinson full-back partnership, which flourished as the season progressed. Unhappily, the financial status of the club was giving cause for concern and the players were further unsettled when everyone, bar Dickinson, was made available for transfer. The future of Portsmouth Football Club at that stage appeared to rest with the vigorous youth scheme being pursued.

Dickinson left for his usual holiday trip to Jersey in the summer. He and Ann visited her parents, with Dickinson only too aware that the team did not have the experience, talent nor depth of understanding to avoid another season of struggle. His summers included regular cricket as a stylish batsman with the Hampshire Maniacs, a club formed by his close friend, Jack Dedman. Golf and tennis always featured on Dickinson's summer agenda and there was the regular pilgrimage to Wimbledon.

That 1960-61 season opened with a surprise when Cox released the highly promising local boy, John Phillips. This followed the controversial pattern set by Cox in allowing the likes of Derek Dougan, Ray Crawford and

Johnny Gordon to leave Fratton Park. Dickinson also said farewell to his old colleague, Reg Flewin. Latterly Pompey's assistant manager, Flewin took over as manager of Stockport County.

Dickinson was forced to break his two-year sequence of continuous appearances when he was 'rested' for the Boxing Day match at Swansea. The apparent reason was the need to protect the veteran from the strain of two matches in successive days and the long journey to Wales. Dickinson was free from playing on either Christmas Day or Boxing Day for the first time in his career. Young full-back Rees Thomas replaced him and Pompey went down 4-0 at Vetch Field.

Dickinson was now using his experience and exceptional ability to 'read' the game to offset his inevitable lack of speed. His former colleagues that season remember a rash remark by Billy Bingham, then a winger with Luton Town. Before a match he pointed at Dickinson and proclaimed, "If I can't outrun him, I'll hang up my boots." The match report shows that Bingham was played out of the game by Pompey's ageing star.

There was a growing feeling within the club that the time was near for Dickinson to be replaced and that, in any event, it was unfair to ask him, however willing he was, to continue to carry such a burden in a struggling side. The first move came from the chairman, Dr McLachlan, in the week after Dickinson had been tormented by Sunderland's speedy winger, Harry Hooper. Dr McLachlan first announced that Dickinson had been offered the post of youth team coach. An hour later came

A night out for the happy couple at a cricket dinner.

48

Jimmy Dickinson tries his hand at ten-pin bowling.

the news that, after 577 League games, he had been dropped for the Saturday home match against Middlesbrough, replaced again by Thomas.

The board were at pains to have Dickinson sit with them in the directors' box and together they saw Brian Clough score a hat-trick as Pompey went down 3-0. It was the first Saturday that Dickinson had watched a Portsmouth first-team match for any reason other than because he was out of the side through injury.

In the three matches in which he had been rested or dropped during Cox's era, Pompey had not scored and had conceded 14 goals. Dickinson looked back on that first-ever omission in later years without any rancour, saying, "We were having a bad time and you couldn't blame the manager for trying every possible combination, could you?"

Normally a club will reward a veteran player nearing the end of his career with the offer of a free transfer. But Dickinson was still considering the special offer made to him when he was promptly reinstated at left-back the following week.

During that season of despair, whilst Cox's position was looking increasingly vulnerable, the maximum wage was removed for professional players and the age of the first £100-a-week footballer had dawned. It was a development which came too late for Dickinson who, in any case, benefited little from the move as wages were inevitably governed by the status of the club concerned.

In February 1961, with relegation almost certain after an appalling sequence when the team won only one of nine home matches, Freddie Cox was finally dismissed. On his departure, Cox had some harsh words to say in the national newspapers about the attitude and co-operation of Pompey's senior players, but it was much more than their intransigence which had led to his downfall. Whatever Dickinson had felt privately about Cox's managership, his loyalty and commitment had never been in question throughout this dark period.

Cox had inherited a club already lacking playing and financial strength, but some ill-judged purchases of footballers from the lower divisions, together with an over-reliance on young players, did not improve his chances.

Whilst a three-man committee of directors ran the team's affairs, there were murmurings in the city that Dickinson might come into the reckoning for the vacant managership. Yet his views on that particular 'hot-seat' were well-known at the club and they gave the directors no encouragement to consider him. The chief scout, Bill Thompson, a former player from the Championship days, took temporary control and immediately secured the services of veteran wing-half Allan Brown, from Luton, and Johnny Gordon, returning to the club after a spell at Birmingham.

As Dickinson approached his 600th League match, the directors were poised to make an inspired appointment. It was one which was to reverse the club's slide and give 36-year-old Dickinson a new lease of football life which would encourage him to play himself into the record books.

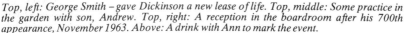

Top, left: George Smith – gave Dickinson a new lease of life. Top, middle: Some practice in the garden with son, Andrew. Top, right: A reception in the boardroom after his 700th appearance, November 1963. Above: A drink with Ann to mark the event.

INDIAN SUMMER WITH SMITH

THE appointment of George Smith on a five-year contract came too late to save Pompey from relegation, but his impact was nevertheless immediate. The Portsmouth Board had been attracted by Smith's reputation as one of the country's leading coaches, particularly for his work at Sheffield United where he had helped the Blades into the First Division and to an FA Cup semi-final. His first acts at Fratton Park were to restore Dickinson to left-half — a position for which he had been considered too old throughout the Cox era — and to reinstate him as captain. Smith and the players were unanimous — it was Dickinson's moral right to be skipper. Smith was adamant, telling reporters, "It seems ridiculous to me that Jimmy should not be leading us."

This unlikely combination — mild-mannered captain and outspoken manager — prospered in the early weeks of Portsmouth's first campaign in the Third Division. A fine team spirit and Pompey's best start to a season since the 1948 Championship win were the portents of a bright

new era at Fratton Park. Smith, who in his way was to be one of the most controversial post-war managers, changed the players from a dispirited set of footballers into a team proud to be reclaiming some of the club's former glories.

Dickinson made a tremendous impression on Smith with his enthusiastic approach to training. The veteran from Alton worked as hard as anyone at Smith's 'commando-style' routines. With his barking sergeant-major's voice, Smith worked the players through a daily course of punishing schedules and Dickinson, haversack full of sand on his back, completed circuits which would have brought players 20 years younger to their knees. Smith's admiration for Pompey's senior player from Alton increased as the season wore on. In several bruising matches the 'know-how' and composure of the experienced half-backs, Brown and Dickinson, proved decisive. Their example inspired the rest of the defence as Pompey opened with a 13-match unbeaten run.

The run took in another milestone for Jimmy Dickinson with his 600th appearance, at home to Barnsley. After Dickinson had been presented with a gold watch from the Supporters' Club and an inscribed bureau from the Football Club, the 16,000 crowd settled down to watch what they hoped would be a match worthy of the occasion. They were to be disappointed for, although Pompey won 3-2, the game was a scrappy affair. Afterwards Dickinson commented, "It is just another match to me. I have never been one to count up appearances although I would love to add a few more yet."

At this point Dickinson was obviously compensating for his age and lack of speed with his fine positional sense and anticipation. Simplicity was now the keynote and the early lay-off to a younger colleague was typical of his 'new' style. The immaculate timing, on the ground and in the air, was still there and his almost telepathic reading of the game more than made up for the fact that he was, inevitably, slowing down.

After that fine opening run, Pompey found themselves at the top of the table by Christmas 1961. Smith had produced a master-stroke with a total outlay of £10,000 on the purchases of two lively wingers in Tony Barton from Nottingham Forest and Dave Dodson from Swansea. Dickinson was thrilled with the enthusiasm of a team, cannily rebuilt by Smith, who were prepared to give everything to get the famous old club out of the Third Division. His enthusiasm was clearly rekindled after it had all but been extinguished by the traumas of the Cox era.

Aided by 26 goals from Ron Saunders and 12 from evergreen Johnny Gordon, and with a resolute defence built around the experience of Snowden, Alex Wilson and Cyril Rutter, Portsmouth won the Third Division championship at the first attempt. Dickinson played in every match and Smith had no doubts about the value of his influence and contribution. "Give me ten other players like this fella," he once announced in Dickinson's embarrassed presence, "and I'll guarantee to win anything in football."

Third Division champions at the first attempt.

As the happy season came to a close, Dickinson gave a clue about his future intentions when he joined colleague Allan Brown on an FA Course for players who wanted to become trainers although, as events turned out, he did not steer himself in that direction. Springtime brought the news that the Dickinsons were expecting their first child after seven years of marriage. Andrew James, who proved to be their only child, was born in hospital in Winchester in October 1962. Ann, a former nurse and midwife, was already well prepared for the rigours of motherhood.

During the 1962-3 season, Jimmy Dickinson continued to confound the pundits. Next to Stanley Matthews he was the oldest League footballer still playing regularly and, for good measure, Pompey's record-breaker was involved in the physical demands of midfield play. George Smith remembered that he insisted on playing in every game. He said, "I couldn't keep him out of the team. He was injured and played — then he strained his groin and played." Even at the age of 38, Dickinson still showed the remarkable resilience and stamina which had marked his play a decade earlier. As before, the bumps, bruises and strains were shaken off with those remarkable recovery and healing qualities.

In the first months of 1962, Britain was plunged into one of the worst winters in living memory. The League and Cup programme was disrupted and there was a frustrating two-month spell of almost total inactivity. Dickinson found himself stranded in Alton, often unable to make his regular journey down to the Portsmouth ground through the country roads of the Meon Valley. It was a difficult season for football in general and Portsmouth in particular, both on the field and financially. In the end Pompey just held their own in the Second Division.

Dickinson enjoyed captaining the side under Smith, due in the main to the mutual respect they had for each other. Dickinson defined his philosophy thus, "The manager is boss at all times except when you are out on the field for those vital 90 minutes on a Saturday. Then the skipper must shoulder the responsibility and must have complete control to cover emergency switches. I accepted the

Below: From left, Bobby Campbell, Roy Lunniss and Dickinson can only watch as Stoke forward Viollet heads past goalkeeper Armstrong.

captaincy on those conditions. The captain must have the full confidence of the team and he must know his players and enough of their background to understand their moods and foibles." All this is something of a contrast to today's teams which are coaxed, cajoled and controlled by animated managers on touchline benches.

Billy Wright, a dear friend and for so long his England colleague, was Dickinson's model. He said, "Billy was the best captain with whom I played. A captain should, by personal effort, encourage his teammates. I'm against any form of bullying. When a player is having a bad time, he does not need to be told — he needs a quiet word of encouragement and assistance. That, to my mind, is real captaincy."

The 1963-4 season was three games old when Dickinson was switched back to centre-half to replace Snowden, this time clearly on a permanent basis. The move was instrumental in extending his playing career even further. At wing-half he was naturally beginning to lose the sharp-edged reactions which had always been so prominent. Moving to the centre of the defence enabled him to make the best use of his keen tactical sense and anticipation allied to his fine tackling.

This was an era when appearance records were of no great concern and it soon became clear that the records were unreliable anyway. This was evident during the early part of the season when the newspapers announced that Dickinson was about to pass the one-club appearance record of Jerry Dawson, a Burnley goalkeeper through two world wars. Dawson had apparently made 693 appearances for the Turf Moor club, but within a few days the same statistical source announced that Dawson's appearances had included wartime football which had to be discounted for Football League record purposes. With Dawson's 'record' now out of the way, it transpired that Dickinson had beaten the official record (held by Harold Bell of Tranmere Rovers with 595 League games) some two years previously in August 1961, without anyone knowing and without any fuss or celebration.

Pompey finished in the top half of the table and the highlight of the season was the passing of yet another milestone with Dickinson's 700th match, against Charlton Athletic. He was an ever-present once again which meant that only once in 16 seasons had he missed more than three League matches in a single campaign, and that only when he suffered his one serious injury. The milestone was greeted with Pompey's best home win of the season, 4-1 on a sea of Fratton Park mud. Dickinson was moved

Cricket with the Hampshire Maniacs club.

by his reception on and off the pitch and on the day he maintained his impeccable standards of poise and precision while around him others floundered. A fascinating duel was fought between Dickinson and the polished centre-forward Eddie Firmani, fresh from his great success playing in Italian football, but it was the veteran centre-half who emerged as the master.

The match remained one of Dickinson's happiest memories and it was the corporate spirit of a team totally committed to the cause of Portsmouth Football Club which meant most to him. He remembered, "We had been having a bad time and Charlton were in an unbeaten run but the lads pulled out all the stops. It stands out in my memories, despite all my caps, despite all the games played and the fine players I played with."

Dickinson and Ron Saunders, with a record 33 goals, were the constant factors of a team which did well to finish in the top half of the table. Supporters were cheered by their side's victory over local rivals Southampton at The Dell, where Pompey won for the first time since 1927. Their 3-2 success was largely a result of one of Dickinson's vintage displays. Despite being the oldest player on the field, his craft and class made him the game's outstanding performer. He played big George Kirby, the Saints' bustling centre-forward, out of the match and showed no signs of flagging in a game of blistering pace and commitment.

Vince Radcliffe, an 18-year-old centre-half, was being groomed to take over from Dickinson but his progress was slow and it began to look as if the club would have to rely on their skipper for yet another season. Even he was made to feel a youngster, however, when Stanley Matthews, close to 50 years of age, teased his old England colleague after enjoying a key role in Stoke City's 4-1 win over Pompey.

By this time George Smith had already made it clear to Dickinson that there was a coaching job waiting for him at Fratton Park when he decided to stop playing. Indeed, Smith was keen to work with him in that form of partnership but the manager's overtures were resisted on two counts. Said Dickinson, "I'm putting no date on the time when I shall finish playing. I judge myself season by season — I'll know when I'm not giving full value for money, no one will need to tell me." On his future plans he reflected the views of his sisters but not necessarily of his wife. "I may get out of football altogether and perhaps open a small business." Ann was not attracted to the prospect of the business venture and, in any event, she knew that her husband would want to stay in the game in some capacity.

In the close season came the accolade set out in the short citation in the Queen's Birthday Honours. 'For services to Association Football: James William Dickinson, Member of the British Empire (MBE).' This was followed by the award of a special commemorative statuette to mark Dickinson's 20 years of playing service. Modestly, the recipient put his longevity down to a lack of quality players pressing to replace him. In his opinion "there is not the quantity of top-class players there were

Dickinson faces up to his last season.

before the war." He was adamant that the player of the 1960s was no more fitter or skilful than his post-war counterpart and that so many players maintained their places due to lack of competition.

The 1964-5 season would turn out to be Dickinson's last as a player and by October, Pompey were at the bottom of the Second Division. Fears were increased with the sale of Saunders to Watford and with the club finances far from healthy, his replacement, Ron Tindall, had to be secured on a free transfer from Reading.

Dickinson's astonishing run of 153 consecutive matches, over three years, ended when young Radcliffe was introduced for a League Cup match at Watford. In the League itself, however, Dickinson was sorely tested as Pompey's defence struggled.

Despite the team's poor showing and the obvious dark period ahead, Dickinson was still undecided about when to call it a day and his future was unclear. He had shown no inclination whatsoever to take up a coaching or training qualification, despite Smith's encouragement, but this was not unexpected in the light of his views on the theorists and tacticians in the game. He had clearly no wish to be a manager, claiming, "It's too precarious for me." If a home was to be found for the man who was 'part of the furniture' at Fratton Park, it would have to be in an administrative role.

At Smith's instigation, the Portsmouth club had been making an effort to 'sell' itself to the public and to 'go after the customers' in an unprecedented move. As part of this effort, and with an eye to Dickinson's future, the player was appointed as a part-time public relations officer, the first such post in League football. Dickinson effectively became a football salesman when he was not training and playing.

He liked the idea at once, feeling that it suited him. Certainly, after overcoming his initial reserve, he got on well with people who were sports-minded. As a result he organised public demonstrations of skill by the players at local halls, backed up by discussion sessions. The club held open days at the ground and asked supporters for suggestions. Features which are commonplace now — but which were novel then — were adopted. There were special seats at Fratton Park for OAPs, transport for out-of-town supporters and even musical record requests before the kick-off.

In the meantime, a desperate fight against relegation was being fought. It was temporarily aided by an eight-match unbeaten run which took Pompey out of the bottom three and which included a 2-2 draw at The Dell in Dickinson's 750th match. The veteran centre-half was by now clearly struggling and a 6-1 defeat at Preston brought this sharply into focus as Dickinson was given a hard time by the strong, physical Alex Dawson. *Linesman* in the local *Football Mail* admitted in his match report that it was "...a sure sign that the years are taking their toll at last."

Within two weeks, in early April 1965, Dickinson had announced that he was retiring at the end of the season. He said, "It's fair to say that, lately, I've been finding it difficult to perform as I want. When weaknesses such as slowness on the turn and speed of recovery appear, then it's time to quit. I would rather retire whilst I am playing a reasonable game than hang on until I'm of no use. That would be a bad way to end."

The enthusiastic Welshman, Harry Harris, was immediately tipped as heir apparent to the captaincy, having operated at left-half without missing a match. Before that, however, Dickinson faced a critical period of four games in seven days as the run-up to his retirement was marked by the now usual dog-fight against relegation over the Easter period.

The first match brought a vital home win over Cardiff City on Easter Saturday, then came the last home match of the season, on Easter Monday against Norwich City.

The historic match — Dickinson's last-ever League game at Fratton Park — saw Pompey win 4-0 to enhance their chances and provide a memorable finale to Dickinson's 22-year playing career on the Portsmouth ground. Fifteen thousand fans gave him a standing ovation as he walked out alone from the tunnel to where the two teams were waiting. Dickinson remembered afterwards how he dreaded the solitary walk to the middle — right to the end he could not bring himself to bask in the limelight.

In that game Dickinson played with all the poise and precision which were his hallmarks. When the final whistle sounded, thousands of fans, in a joyous outburst unrestricted by fencing, followed him around the ground on his personal lap of honour. The champagne flowed in the dressing-room and Alf Ramsey led the celebrations. Smith summed up the team's performance on that special day thus: "The greatest compliment paid to Jimmy today was the way in which the team played for him."

The following day, Portsmouth travelled to Norwich for the return match and Smith sprang a major surprise by omitting Dickinson for the first time, feeling that he needed a break after two games in three days. With hindsight it was a tactical error and Dickinson admitted that he had not been hard-pressed in either of the previous games. In the event, Radcliffe, at centre-half for his League debut, was outsmarted by the experienced Ron Davies, who was later to play for Southampton with great distinction. Pompey's 3-1 defeat at Carrow Road, after they had beaten the Canaries so convincingly the day before, meant that the last relegation place would be decided by the last match.

The result of that final game would make or mar the retirement of one of the greatest club loyalists football has ever produced. For Dickinson's legions of admirers there was so much more than survival in the Second Division hanging on this match.

Before his last home match against Norwich. Harry Harris makes a presentation on behalf of the team to the captain.

THE GRAND FINALE

IF it had been possible to write the script, then Jimmy Dickinson would have played his last and 764th League match — on his 40th birthday for good measure — at Wembley, White Hart Lane or Highbury, with his beloved Pompey poised to win another Cup Final or League Championship.

Instead it was the unlikely venue of the County Ground at Northampton on a balmy Saturday evening in late April where the prize to be gained was the point which would prevent Pompey falling back into the Third Division. The essential qualities which go to make a top football stadium are certainly not at Northampton and of all the grounds in the Football League, the Cobblers' home must be one of the least 'atmospheric'. The ground is shared with the County Cricket Club and opposite the tiny and cramped 'cowshed' stand stood the cricket scoreboard with that side of the ground devoid of terracing. No sweeping banking adorns this venue and only a small hummock gave any semblance of a Spion Kop.

None of that mattered to the 20,000 local fans who gathered to salute Northampton's first-ever promotion to Division One. With no chance of taking the title from Newcastle, but with an unbeaten home record to preserve, those supporters were already planning their celebrations after the formality of a banker home win.

Pompey, for their part, had won only one away match all season but as they made their way to Northampton,

Dickinson and his team were encouraged by the result from Southampton that afternoon where Terry Paine had done his neighbours a favour by scoring a late winner against Swindon Town. This left Pompey level on points with Swindon but with an inferior goal-average meaning that at least one point was required for safety.

It was to be an agonising night for Pompey fans after Dickinson had been applauded on to the field by both teams. Without the benefit of local or national radio coverage, hordes of supporters in the Portsmouth area descended on various local newspaper offices to keep abreast of the proceedings from reporters' regular telephone calls.

At first Portsmouth stunned the home crowd with their excellent approach work, but again they were plagued by their inability to capitalise on such creativity and the commentators were agreed that Pompey should have been at least one goal to the good by half-time. As the match drifted into the last quarter, it seemed that a goalless draw might be the outcome as Northampton showed no real appetite to spoil Dickinson's evening.

What seemed to be the cruellest blow of all came some 13 minutes from the end. The Cobblers' defence trapped three Portsmouth forwards offside and the resultant free-kick was lobbed into the Pompey goalmouth. Up went defenders and attackers alike and the ball flew off the top of Johnny Gordon's head and into the net out of

the reach of goalkeeper John Armstrong. There was little applause from the surprised crowd who knew that Pompey and their skipper did not deserve to be so shabbily treated by fate. Gordon, that devoted servant of Pompey over the years, was mortified. He said later, "I thought that Pompey supporters would blame me for the rest of their lives and if we had lost by that goal I would have walked home from Northampton and given up the game."

As the last few minutes of Jimmy Dickinson's great playing career ticked away, it seemed that nothing could prevent Pompey from defeat and relegation. Six minutes were left when fate redeemed itself. John McClelland took a corner for Pompey on the right and the whole Portsmouth team, bar the goalkeeper, poured forward and camped in and around the penalty area. Harry Harris got his head to the ball, Cliff Portwood touched it on and it fell so invitingly for full-back Alex Wilson to hammer in a shot which sneaked through the crowded goalmouth and hit a defender on its way into the corner of the net.

Top, far left: Dickinson takes the field to a welcome from both teams at Northampton.
Top, centre: The goalscorers Gordon and Wilson chair Dickinson from the field.
Above: Harry Harris, next to Dickinson, and John McClelland re-live the match-saving goal.
Bottom: Dickinson, flanked by Johnny Gordon (left) and Alex Wilson, celebrate the 'Great Escape' at Northamton.

Wilson, who had previously scored only one League goal in more than 250 appearances remembered, "I couldn't believe it when I hit the ball and saw it end up in the net."

So Pompey got their point and Jimmy Dickinson was carried shoulder-high from the field with no unhappy shadow to mar his retirement. In the dressing-room mayhem he had time to say, "I couldn't have finished my career on a better note. Things rarely work out as you hope they will, but they've done so for me today. It's the finest thing which has happened to me in football."

DEBUT

WHEN the Football Association decided to undertake the most ambitious tour in its history in May 1949, when five countries were to be visited in the space of ten days through Scandinavia, Holland and France, it was natural that the selectors should look towards the League Champions, even if it was only a glance. Thus, Jimmy Dickinson received recognition for his magnificent club season and was included in the 26-strong party. There was still disappointment in Portsmouth, however, when Peter Harris, Len Phillips and Jack Froggatt were overlooked. Despite their dismay, Pompey's supporters were not greatly surprised, for their club had never been regarded as a 'fashionable' outfit. Even the Championship-winning team had not drawn the acclaim they deserved.

Walter Winterbottom, the England team manager, had been on the look-out for young players to replace his pre-war veterans. He was attracted to the young Portsmouth wing-half, who seemed the likeliest candidate for grooming into the 'ball-winner' his defence needed. Dickinson's high level of consistency throughout that Championship season convinced Winterbottom and his fellow selectors that here was a player who could be relied upon to produce his best in every game.

Coincidentally, Pompey themselves were embarking on a tour of Sweden and Denmark as the FA party's two aircraft took off for Stockholm. Dickinson expected to be in the 'B' party and watched the full side lose 3-1 in their opening match against Sweden, the Olympic champions. Next day the 'B' team flew to Helsinki and on Finland's hottest day of the year, Dickinson excelled in a 4-0 win. His performance behind the three 'M's' — Morris, Mannion and Mullen — was enough to persuade the selectors to promote him to the senior squad which was about to fly to Oslo.

On 18 May 1949, with the King of Norway and the Crown Prince in attendance, Jimmy Dickinson began his senior international career as left-half replacement for Henry Cockburn of Manchester United. A heavy thunderstorm broke over the ground in the afternoon but the sun was shining by the time the game kicked-off at six o'clock. It was a comfortable debut, despite the slippery ground and greasy ball, and proved little more than an exhibition game as England cantered to an easy 4-1 victory.

Dickinson earned warm praise from the Press. One report told of "a perfect attacking game so quick in recovery that John Aston behind had not a moment's worry". He was reckoned to be the best of the three new caps — Bill Ellerington of Southampton and Johnny Morris of Derby being the other debutants. Dickinson's debut had coincided with the last international appearance of the great goalkeeper Frank Swift, who had just announced his retirement. Winterbottom remembers that the Pompey man hit it off immediately with his fellow defenders, Neil Franklin and Billy Wright, an aspect which particularly encouraged the England manager. For the record that England team lined up, Swift; Ellerington,

Peter Harris, Dickinson and Tom Finney with Walter Winterbottom (left) and the chairman of selectors, Arthur Drewry, before the international against the Republic of Ireland in September, 1949.

Aston; Wright, Franklin, Dickinson; Finney, Morris, Mortensen, Mannion, Mullen.

Jimmy Dickinson was now an automatic choice for the last game of the tour, a stiff test against France at the

The young man from Alton makes his point at one of the attendant social functions.

Colombes Stadium in Paris, four days later. The 'B' squad had left for home and the senior party suffered a bumpy flight *en route* to the French capital. The magnificent stadium, bathed in sunshine on a hot, sultry afternoon, presented the players with a hard pitch with little grass which resembled an unfriendly pavement. They were trying conditions for the nervous youngster from Alton, concluding a hectic ten days of flying and playing international football.

The 65,000 partisan crowd in their gayest colours were ecstatic when a mistake by goalkeeper Bert Williams gifted a goal to the French after only 25 seconds. It was the quickest goal ever scored against England and Jimmy Dickinson, so mature in only his second international, more than anyone pulled them through a difficult period after that. The Press certainly were in no doubt, "A place of honour to Dickinson for a tireless and intelligent display .... experienced men like Franklin, Wright and Aston owed Dickinson a great deal."

The equaliser came after a delightful movement involving Dickinson and Jack Rowley and completed by Morris. England finished 3-1 winners, a victory marked by a first England goal for Billy Wright. It was clear that Jimmy Dickinson, one of the stars of the trip, had stiffened the half-back line and looked to have played his way into the England team for a long time to come.

The shy, slightly withdrawn young man from Alton was initially out of his depth in the company of the experienced professionals in the England party and at the attendant social functions. He was soon taken under the wing of the more outgoing Billy Wright, a fellow defender with whom he was to share a room throughout his England career. He was to forge a lifelong friendship with the blond Wolves stalwart who, off the field was a delightful,

unassuming and entirely gentle person who loved classical music. Wright was to go on to captain his country and become the first Englishman to win 100 international caps. Dickinson, meanwhile, had come to like and admire Walter Winterbottom, reflecting that the FA's chief coach, drawing on his pipe, looked like a schoolmaster or even a scientist.

Although thrilled at the outcome of his first taste of international football, Jimmy Dickinson was relieved to leave the pressures of the tour and rejoin his Pompey colleagues in Copenhagen for the remainder of their Denmark trip. Much as he was always proud of his international involvement, Dickinson liked nothing better than to return to the day-to-day company and routines of his friends at club level. Not that they would ever be made aware that he had been in exalted company. His reticence was such that very little of his international experiences would be recounted to them except by tortuous extraction.

It was a pleasure for Dickinson to have Peter Harris for company in the first international of 1949-50, when Harris gained his first cap at outside-right. In the event, it was an unpleasant shock for England as the match against the Republic of Ireland at Goodison Park was lost 2-0. It was the Republic's first international appearance in England and they can still claim that they were the first 'foreign' side to beat England on English soil.

The defeat did not enhance the reputation of the two Portsmouth players and Harris, much to Dickinson's regret, was not to get another chance in an England shirt for almost five years. In truth, defeat by Eire had less to do with that than the presence of the incomparable Stanley Matthews and Tom Finney on the wings.

The Home International Championship, now defunct, was then a focus for national pride and England won the title with maximum points in 1949-50. Their success was even more significant because the Championship doubled up as a World Cup qualifying competition with the winners gaining one of the 16 places in the Finals in Brazil that summer. After playing in the 4-1 win over Wales at Cardiff — England's victory was due largely to a hat-trick by Newcastle's Jackie Milburn — Dickinson was not selected for the next two internationals and feared for his place.

The blow was softened when he was selected to captain England 'B' for two matches and by the general feeling in the Press that the two matches for which he was omitted were being used by the selectors to look at other players for the World Cup party. One of these was Jack Froggatt from Portsmouth, who despite scoring in a 9-2 win over Northern Ireland, did not get another England chance for two years — and then at centre-half for 13 matches.

In those days there were few arguments over club or country loyalty when it came to selecting England teams, despite the fact that international matches were often played on a Saturday when a full First Division programme went ahead regardless. If Pompey were depleted by the loss of Dickinson and Jack Froggatt to England and perhaps Jimmy Scoular for Scotland, then they had to make do as best they could.

Dickinson was thrilled to be recalled for the annual fixture between Scotland and England in April 1950 and with the World Cup Finals just two months away, this was also to be the deciding match of the British World Cup qualifying section. Curiously, the original idea was that the Home Championship runners-up would also qualify for the World Cup but Scotland, in a mood of arrogance, announced that they would travel to Brazil only if they won the title.

For Dickinson, stepping out at Hampden Park, Glasgow, for the first time since his appearance there almost six years earlier in the ATC international, it was the supreme test of his talent and composure. This time the crowd numbered 138,000 and whether the football be good or bad, the atmosphere at Hampden Park when England are the visitors is an unforgettable experience for a footballer. In the 1950s, in particular, the matches were played against an intense emotional background and were an immense physical and mental strain on the players.

Dickinson recalled that as he walked out into the amphitheatre of Scotland's national stadium, he was immediately aware that the 'Hampden Roar' was no myth. They said it could be heard ten miles from the ground and inside the stadium its impact upon the senses was almost painful. He was moved by the strident, colourful Scottish crowd with their kilts, tartan bonnets and bagpipes, but the 'Roar' became a whisper as England sneaked a goal midway through the second half. Dickinson began the move with a pass down the left to Bobby Langton, who found Roy Bentley in a opening to shoot past Cowan. The last 15 minutes were of blinding excitement climaxed by the save of a lifetime from Bert Williams, who took the ball at full stretch from a volley by Billy Liddell.

Dickinson's play was a decisive factor in England's victory and he kept Finney and Mortensen supplied with a flow of passes. When the Scots, with their tricky forwards, threatened they found life difficult against Dickinson's covering and determined tackling.

As runners-up to England, the Scots had to live up to their promise and were forced to withdraw from the World Cup, much to the amazement of Jimmy Dickinson and the England contingent. Dickinson's appetite for contests against Scotland was aroused by that match and he would look forward eagerly to future matches between the two countries, reserving some of his best performances for them.

His England place was now assured and there was now just one thing to occupy his mind over the ensuing weeks — his first visit to South America and England's first challenge for the World Cup. The FA squeezed in two friendlies by way of preparation before the England party departed for Brazil. The first, in Lisbon, was won 5-3 with Tom Finney, who scored two penalties, in brilliant form although the nippy Portuguese forwards gave Dickinson plenty to do in defence. In Brussels, an easy 4-1 victory over Belgium was an altogether more comfortable experience for the young Pompey wing-half.

By this time England had played more than 30 internationals since the war, losing only four. With those sound credentials they were rated amongst the favourites for the World Cup. The credit for much of their success lay with the tall, compelling Walter Winterbottom who, in the post-war years, brought English international football in line with developments abroad. Jimmy Dickinson always recognised Winterbottom as a theorist who was in a class of his own. But while Dickinson was fond of the man, like some of his fellow players he often found him too erudite. Tactically, Winterbottom was way ahead of his time and the players could not — or would not — always respond.

Jimmy Dickinson (centre) with Billy Wright, Tom Finney and the skating stars who visited Wembley in the early 1950s.

Among Winterbottom's aims was the encouragement of quick thinking and the speeding up of players' reactions. Dickinson and his colleagues often found themselves sitting in hotel lounges while Winterbottom thought up games designed to promote nimble minds. This mental stimulation would, Winterbottom hoped, enable players to absorb fully the contents of the manager's team-talks as he methodically dissected the opposition. As far as Dickinson was concerned, this constituted a radical change from the pre-match preparations at Portsmouth.

The FA's director of coaching was not in sole charge of the team and selection lay with a 12-man committee, who would discuss each position in turn and vote if necessary. Dickinson was a player who Winterbottom would always have had in the side, but the team he fielded was not always of his choosing, even if he had tried to wield some influence.

For England, meanwhile, the World Cup Finals were the first truly competitive test for the country which had given the game to the world at large. For too long the English had been an insular football nation. Now their ageing squad — 25-year-old Jimmy Dickinson was the youngest — were to learn to their cost of the progress of the world's footballing countries. And they were to receive a shock from a most unexpected source.

IV CAMPEONATO
MUNDIAL DE
FUTEBOL

·TAÇA JULES RIMET·

BRASIL
JUNHO DE 1950

Contra dores
CAFIASPIRINA BAYER
·O remedio de confianca·

The cover of the programme for the Finals in Brazil.

WORLD CUP HUMILIATION

IT was the greatest football upset of all time. A giant-killing act so incredible that newspaper sub-editors around the world thought it was a typing error when the score came through on teleprinter and tape machines: USA 1 England 0 — surely it must be 1-10 to England? Soon, however, the sensation was confirmed on radio. For the rest of his life Jimmy Dickinson would continually be faced with the embarrassment of having been a part of the humiliation and just as often be at a loss to explain it away. As Billy Wright, the England centre-half admitted,

"It was a bit like the MCC being beaten by Germany at cricket."

The biggest shock that English football had ever suffered occurred in the World Cup Finals in Brazil in June 1950, a year after Dickinson's international debut. It happened in a little stadium, which looked more like a bullring than a football ground, in Belo Horizonte, a goldmining community high in the mountains, 300 miles from Rio. On a bumpy pitch, England suffered the humiliation of a single-goal defeat by the United States of America. A team of American soccer players, eight of whom were born and bred in the States, shrugged off the effects of a party the night before and stole a goal just before half-time. The Americans, who worked at everyday jobs through the week and played football for pleasure on Sunday afternoons, achieved an historic victory, aided by some woeful finishing by the England forwards.

The Times reported, "Never before has an England team played so badly......the chances they missed were legion......with the American goal at their mercy they blazed over the bar or hesitated fatally near goal." For the most part, Jimmy Dickinson could only stand and watch in disbelief from a redundant defensive position. Astonishingly, England hit the woodwork no less than 11 times in all. Dickinson forgot himself in his frustration and moved forward to hammer a fine shot which went just wide. It was alleged to be only the third shot he had produced at international level.

The story of that upset has been told many times. English newspapers headlined doom and shame for days and sports pages all over the world carried pictures of the American goalscorer, a Haitian called Joe Gaetjens, being carried aloft from the field by excited Brazilian fans who had crowded into the ground on that humid, cloudy afternoon expecting to see England massacre the Americans. Strangely, the stunning achievement was largely ignored by newspapers in the USA.

England, together with host country Brazil, were generally regarded as the favourites — Brazil as a skilful, naturally talented team playing with home advantage, England because they boasted such world-famous footballers as Matthews, Finney, Mannion, Wright and Ramsey. Certainly the South Americans knew far more about the reputations of the English players than Dickinson and the rest of the England party knew about their opponents.

The general feeling at home was that England's participation in the World Cup for the first time gave the competition a status it did not deserve at the time. The *Portsmouth Football Mail* correspondent 'Ranger' summed up this attitude, "There is a feeling amongst those most closely associated with the game that competitive football amongst various countries of the world can develop into very unpleasant affairs — certain people feel that England should withdraw from the competition." Whether such an opinion had been elicited from Dickinson before his departure we shall never know.

The flight to Rio de Janeiro was 'big news' in the Brazilian capital. Occasional flashes were put over the radio that the 'Kings of Football' were within a certain distance of the airport. When the England party touched down, they were met by what was described as the largest crowd of reporters, photographers and radio journalists ever to greet a football team. There followed two hours of interviews which left the England players hoarse after shouting above the din. It was quite a culture shock for Jimmy Dickinson to realise that the South Americans were mad about football in a way that a simple Alton boy with a somewhat insular outlook could scarcely imagine. Later, he was to be amazed at the volatile nature of the crowds, the attendant fireworks and flares and the then unusual sight of fences separating spectators and players.

In later years he was to reflect upon the England party's appalling lack of preparation which saw them arrive in the charge of sole selector and FA chairman, Arthur Drewry, and the director of coaching, Walter Winterbottom, in an unfamiliar continent with only five days acclimatization after just four days together in England prior to departure. The South American teams, meanwhile, had been together for many months, free from competitive club football. In contrast, Dickinson had just completed a long English season of over 50 League and Cup matches.

Typical of the lack of preparation which Dickinson ruefully remembered was a disregard for suitable medical cover for the inevitable health hazards. A local doctor was quickly recruited and his first task was to supply the Portsmouth man with sleeping tablets to offset the effects of fire-crackers which were thrown at the windows of England's hotel. The Luxor Hotel had been recommended to Winterbottom by Tom Whittaker, the Arsenal manager.

The Gunners might have once enjoyed a stay there but it was a disaster for England, whose rooms were situated near a noisy lift which operated all night to the kitchens.

Dickinson and his good friend and room-mate, Billy Wright, enjoyed the location of the party's Luxor Hotel which was alongside the famous Copacabana beach, world-famous as the playground of the rich. However, Winterbottom was only too aware of the dangers of sunstroke and the players were forbidden to venture on to the tempting sands. Wright remembers,"Before us was the kind of scene we had conjured up in our minds after seeing 'Flying down to Rio' with Fred Astaire and Ginger Rogers. When Walter Winterbottom informed us that the beach was out of bounds, though, I felt I might as well be in my own back garden as in the South American paradise." Cossetted in the hotel under the watchful eye of the Brazilian doctor, not to mention the restraints imposed by the meagre £2 per-day pocket money, the England players were never in any danger of moral laxity. Another disappointment was the food. The Brazilian notion of an 'English breakfast' was eggs cooked in black oil and bacon of rather dubious origin. Not for the first time, Winterbottom went to the kitchen and sought out the chef in order to show him just how English footballers liked their food prepared.

Botofogo, one of the leading Brazilian clubs, placed their training facilities at England's disposal and every session

Jimmy Dickinson, trainer Bill Riddings, Billy Wright and Bill Nicholson examine a pair of lightweight 'Rio Boots'

was attended by hundreds of locals, gaping, hanging around in groups, talking excitedly. Every piece of action, every little movement was a subject for comment as they caught their first glimpse of the masters from the country that gave football to the world.

Dickinson managed to fit in some games of tennis with members of the English colony and made quite an impression with his game. Jack Archer, then of the *Sunday People,* tells an amusing story of a chance meeting with one of their number many years later. He told Archer about Dickinson's impact at the tennis club "When we invited him to play, he was head and shoulders above the rest — young Dickinson was the greatest tennis player they sent out there." When Archer told him that Dickinson had received an MBE for his services to the game, back came the retort, "Jolly good for him, I always knew he would do well at Wimbledon."

England were placed in Pool Two with Chile, Spain and the United States. The first and third matches were played at the massive three-tiered, then uncompleted Maracana Stadium in Rio, which boasted magnificent floodlights. England were invited to take advantage of the lights and play in the cool of the evening but declined, stubbornly insisting on turning out in the heat of the Brazilian day.

After an undistinguished 2-0 win over Chile, England travelled to their camp 16 miles from Belo Horizonte, where they were guests of a local mining company. The camp was reached along a road which appeared to cling to the side of the hills and Dickinson counted 167 hairpin bends which had to be negotiated. Once installed, the England players enjoyed many comforts, including facilities for swimming, cricket and snooker, and there was a complacent air about their preparation in the mountains.

As the team, already changed, travelled down in their bus they could not have imagined the disaster that awaited them. The Brazilian Press saw England winning "wearing bowler hats and carrying umbrellas without raising any perspiration". After the humiliation Dickinson remembered those same newspapers being burned on the terraces, a funeral pyre for England and their hopes.

His reaction to the defeat was typical. Like the rest of the English players he took it like the archetypal English gentleman. The American manager, Chubby Lyons, remembered, "They congratulated us, though I knew how they must have felt. They showed that stiff upper lip which Hitler could never understand." For Dickinson, though, there was the memory of some extremely poor refereeing — once Mortensen clearly had the ball over line before the goalkeeper clawed it away — and the crowd hanging on to the ball for long periods with no allowance made on the referee's watch.

England returned to Rio for their final Pool match, knowing that victory over Spain was their only hope if they were to reach the next stage. Out went Aston, Mullen, Mannion and Bentley; in came Matthews, Baily, Eckersley and Milburn. The changes were in vain, however, and despite applying continuous pressure England again went

down 1-0. The FA party immediately packed their bags and began the 6,000-mile journey home. There were plenty of excuses — the foreigners were too fond of dubious tactics such as obstruction, the referees were of poor standard, the climate was against England and so on. The fact remained that the team had been ill-prepared, both practically and mentally.

A major factor, according to Dickinson, had been the extreme humidity. Oxygen had been made available at half-time and the Portsmouth man, who was having

difficulty with his breathing, tried a whiff without being impressed by its effect. Long before the final whistle of each game, Dickinson had felt utterly drained of energy.

English football had paid the price for its insularity. At home the World Cup was still regarded as something which only foreigners got worked up about. Nevertheless it was a chastening experience for Jimmy Dickinson, although at least his reputation was still intact, unlike those of some of his older, more illustrious colleagues.

It says much for England's attitude that they flew back to London the day after being eliminated. Had they stayed to watch the later stages of the competition and the glorious World Cup Final between Brazil and Uruguay, they may well have learned something which could have prevented the disasters just three years away.

The goal that shook the world. United States centre-forward Gaetjens puts the ball past England goalkeeper Bert Williams in the World Cup game at Belo Horizonte, in which America beat England 1-0 to the amazement of soccer fans everywhere.

CHALLENGES FROM

The England party embark on their continental tour to Italy, Austria and Switzerland – May 1952. Dickinson is standing in the g

his mackintosh.

T HE post-mortem over, the 1950-51 season opened with the Home countries facing a difficult time in the international arena. The World Cup had shown clearly what type of football was developing and word was spreading about the strength of the Central European sides. A more scientific approach was soon apparent and Jimmy Dickinson — to his amusement because he was never to be convinced of the value of planned coaching — was conscious of sophisticated training schemes rather than the dull, repetitive physical routines to which he had been accustomed. Winterbottom's international reputation was built around his detailed study of the game, on his ability to chart and analyse.

Dickinson retained his place for the Home internationals against Ireland and Wales but after playing in the 2-2 draw against Yugoslavia at Highbury, a friendly international marked by two goals from debutant Nat Lofthouse, he was disappointed to lose his place for the Scotland match at Wembley. His omission was as a result of an unusually poor game for the Football League against the Irish League the previous week. England had to solve a centre-half problem after the 'defection' of Stoke City's Neil Franklin to South America, in search of riches with the Santa Fe club of Bogotá. Ironically, the England number-five shirt was given to Dickinson's club colleague, Jack Froggatt, for the match which the Scots won 3-2.

Froggatt's selection was a remarkable achievement. Only three months before, he had made the unusual switch from outside-left to centre-half for Portsmouth when Flewin had fallen ill. So well did he adapt to his new role, with his strength and speed into the tackle, that England could not overlook him. He was the first player since 1900 to appear in two separate 'departments' of the England team. Froggatt introduced something new to modern centre-half play with his attacking tendencies — it was, of course, a feature of the game before the 'stopper' was invented — although it meant that Dickinson had to be extra vigilant to cover for him. Froggatt, with his speed going forward and his ability to recover quickly, brought a new dimension to the Pompey side.

The selectors overlooked Dickinson for the next three internationals, which were planned as part of the Festival of Britain. Instead they recalled Manchester United's veteran wing-half, Henry Cockburn, whose international career appeared to have ended with Dickinson's arrival on the scene. Jimmy Dickinson, meanwhile, took off with Pompey on their South American tour.

Early in 1951-2, Dickinson gave a fine display for the Football League in their 9-1 win over the Irish League. The selectors were convinced and along with Eddie Baily and Les Medley of Spurs, Dickinson was recalled against Wales to form a new left-wing triangle. It worked well and England drew 1-1 in Cardiff. Two weeks later Dickinson and Len Phillips played against the Scottish League and both did well enough to earn a place in the full international side to meet Northern Ireland at Villa Park in November 1951. It was to be Phillips' only cap and it was a pity that he did not show more of his undoubted talent. Dickinson was conscious that his Pompey colleague was working too deep and was not creative enough in attack to impress the selectors. Two years later Phillips was back in the England reckoning but injury prevented him getting another chance.

Dickinson's return to the England scene saw him take part in one of the truly great matches of the post-war years — Austria's first visit to Wembley. Austria had beaten Scotland home and away and Dickinson knew that England faced a stiff task. Nevertheless, he was surprised when the players were called together two days before the match and practised on a scale never previously attempted. His anticipation of a magnificent contest was not misplaced. The Austrians were the uncrowned champions of Europe and came to Wembley with a great reputation which was to be enhanced by their superb technique.

Jimmy Dickinson had one of his finest matches in an England shirt and the game also saw a good display by Jack Froggatt. The pair did the Pompey supporters in

Goalkeeper Merrick safely gathers the ball under Dickinson's watchful gaze against Switzerland in Zurich, May 1952.

The England team which met Wales, November 1952. Back (left to right): Lofthouse, Ramsey, Merrick, Smith, Dickinson, J. Froggatt. Front: Finney, R. Froggatt, Wright, Bentley and Elliott.

the crowd proud, tackling like lions and covering nearly every blade of the lush Wembley turf as they shadowed the interchanging Austrian forwards. Dickinson's positional sense was uncanny. His creativity was quite superb and the left-wing pair of Eddie Baily and Les Medley posed continual problems for the Austrian defence as the result of Dickinson's prompting.

For all the efforts of the Pompey duo, England's defence struggled to cope with the skilful Austrian ball-players, who seemed to possess a deeper knowledge of the game than their rivals. England retained their unbeaten home record against teams from outside the British Isles with a 2-2 draw, but it was a close thing.

In April, England beat Scotland 2-1 at Hampden Park. It was a particularly proud day for Pompey as they supplied their entire half-back line. Jimmy Scoular, Scotland's right-half, was the outstanding home player on view; and Froggatt and Dickinson for England helped engineer a memorable victory.

England made ready for their summer tour and Jimmy Dickinson looked forward to the trip. International travel had increased his confidence and he had developed into a good mixer amongst people who would talk sport. He would always be a private person and no one would ever get really close to him. Yet people liked him, however slight their acquaintance — not only for the man himself but also for what he stood for.

The tour started with a 1-1 draw against Italy in Florence and ended with a 3-0 win against Switzerland in Zürich. The first game was remembered by Dickinson as a rough, bruising match in which a nasty incident was averted only by the quick thinking of some Italian players. After Lofthouse and an Italian defender had gone into a tackle, some of the crowd began throwing bottles on to the pitch. Six Italian footballers went over and remonstrated with the trouble-makers.

The highlight of the tour, however, was the eagerly-awaited return against Austria in Vienna. The match in the Prater Stadium, in the Russian sector of the still-divided war-torn city, was an intensely emotional affair. Some 2,000 seats had been reserved for the Russians but none came. There were, however, 2,000 British servicemen in the 60,000 crowd and they gave massive vocal support and were rewarded by a superb individual goal from Nat Lofthose which won the match. With the score at 2-2, Lofthouse embarked upon a 50-yard run, urged on by the British tommies, and ended it by sliding the ball home before colliding with the goalkeeper. It was a memory which would remain with Dickinson for the rest of his life. The injured Lofthouse was carried off and as the minutes ticked away, hundreds of British soldiers went delirious. Dickinson, trying to take a throw-in, found himself stepping on piles of sausages strewn along the touchline after an excited soldier knocked a tray out of an Austrian vendor's hands.

England's half-backs, Wright, Froggatt and Dickinson, were the mainspring of this fine victory. At the final whistle, hundreds of khaki-clad British servicemen poured on to the pitch and carried off the red-shirted England players

68

shoulder-high. They looked, according to one writer, like poppies in a cornfield. After the game, England were hailed as 'European champions' by some sections of the Press and the FA were so pleased with the result that they presented every member of the party with a £40 bonus.

The 1952-3 international season saw Nat Loftfouse, now dubbed 'The Lion of Vienna', maintain his scoring record and England shared the Home Championship after drawing in Belfast and beating Wales 5-2 at Wembley. The issue was decided at Wembley, when Scotland earned a 2-2 draw in one of the most exciting of all matches between the old enemies.

Jimmy Dickinson had a new partner when Malcolm Barrass of Bolton was capped at centre-half. Jack Froggatt returned to the left-wing, to be partnered by his cousin, Redfern Froggatt of Sheffield Wednesday. Dickinson acknowledged that this was probably his finest match at Wembley but he could not prevent a ten-man Scotland team equalising in injury-time. The late Roy Peskett, a founder member of the Football Writers' Association,

wrote, "Dickinson was simply outstanding in defence and attack, pinpointing passes in uncanny style and switching the play disconcertingly." Many of us who watched Dickinson in later years, when he was used in a purely defensive role, were unaware of his creativity and passing talents when he was at his peak. He capped his fine display at Wembley that April day in 1953 by making a superb clearance off his own goal-line after goalkeeper Gil Merrick was beaten. Dickinson, on his knees, somehow got to the ball to head it away.

Jimmy Dickinson was now at his peak. Only Duncan Edwards, Bobby Moore and Bryan Robson would join him in a list of the greatest England left-sided midfield players since the war. The triple factors of England's return to FIFA, the increase in air-travel and the Football Association's sudden desire to tackle the best teams in the world, had brought about a dramatic widening of Dickinson's football horizons.

Nat Lofthouse challenges Rest of the World goalkeeper Zeman at Wembley in 1953.

By now Dickinson's name was almost the first to be pencilled in by Winterbottom and the other selectors. While they felt that the Pompey man had no great turn of speed, Winterbottom valued his superb anticipation and uncanny 'reading' of the game. A bonus was Dickinson's calm approach to international football. According to Winterbottom, only Alf Ramsey and Stan Matthews could match his cool. Dickinson and Wright, in particular, were detailed to look after less experienced members of the England party and Dickinson would often share a room with a newcomer to the full international scene.

The summer of that Coronation Year took him off on his longest jaunt so far — a visit to North and South America as a prelude to the forthcoming World Cup qualifying rounds. The 25,000-mile journey was via Madrid, Dakar (West Africa) to Rio, Buenos Aires, Santiago, Montevideo, Port of Spain and, finally, New York.

A practice match against a Buenos Aires XI was lost 3-1 and, although the game did not rank as an international, the result was a real shock for the tourists, who were not surprised when the Buenos Aires team was selected *en bloc* to represent Argentina three days later.

A rain-storm flooded the ground an hour before kick-off and although loads of sawdust was dumped on the pitch, it still resembled a lake. In the most farcical conditions Dickinson had ever encountered, the players were so covered in mud that they could hardly be recognised. Mercifully, the game was abandoned after 22 minutes with no score. There was no time in the tour's schedule for the match to be replayed, so the prestige at stake was unresolved.

The previous day, Billy Wright and Dickinson helped carry a wreath at a service in the city for Eva Peron, who had died during their visit. Dickinson would return from the tour and recount his introduction to Juan Peron, the Argentinian Premier. Later still he jokingly referred to it as a glaring omission from the script of the musical,

'Evita'. The party were again disturbed by the passionate and sometimes hostile South American crowds. Dickinson often recalled the day in Argentina when England's team 'bus was surrounded by hundreds of fans, who bombarded the vehicle with small oranges. It was a frightening experience for the occupants of the coach.

After a convincing victory over a moderate Chile side in Santiago, England lost 2-1 in a testing match against Uruguay in Montevideo. The reigning World Champions outplayed their visitors and Dickinson conceded that the Uruguayans were the most physical and strongest team he had ever met. Their inside-forwards, particularly the brilliant Schiaffino, tormented Dickinson and his fellow defenders, Wright and Harry Johnston of Blackpool. The Uruguayan forwards gave notice to Dickinson of what was to be in store for him in the 1954 World Cup.

On the way home, England wound up the tour with a match in the New York Yankees' stadium, where their 6-3 victory over the USA proved some consolation for the humiliation of the World Cup defeat by the Americans three years earlier. It was the first time that a full England team — and Dickinson himself — had played under floodlights. It was also one of the smallest attendances which the Portsmouth man had played before — only 7,721 saw England's first visit to the USA for a full international. Afterwards, the FA party visited Broadway, the Empire State Building and Radio City.

The return from the tiring tour marked the end of an 18-month period of almost continuous football for Jimmy Dickinson, taking in two League seasons, plus 15 consecutive internationals which included tours to Europe and the Americas, not to mention FA Cup and inter-League matches.

Despite England's international decline in football, they had never been beaten by a foreign team on their own soil. The day of reckoning was getting perilously close, however, and Jimmy Dickinson was to be very much involved.

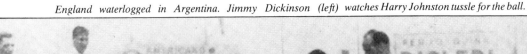

England waterlogged in Argentina. Jimmy Dickinson (left) watches Harry Johnston tussle for the ball.

Above: Walter Winterbottom talks tactics with (from left): Bill Eckersley, Leslie Compton, Jimmy Dickinson, Willie Watson and Alj Ramsey.
Below: 'Smile, please.' Dickinson is lined up by a cameraman in Florence before England's game against Italy.

The line-up against Wales, October 1953. Back (left to right): Lofthouse, Johnston, Merrick, Garrett, Dickinson, Eckersley, Finney. Front: Quixall, Wright, Wilshaw and Mullen.

A reunion at Wembley for 'Monty' and Dickinson before the international against the Rest of Europe, October 1953. Ufton and Ramsey are on Dickinson's left.

The line-up for the Hungary debacle at Wembley, November 1953. Back (left to right): Ramsey, Wright, Merrick, Johnston, Dickinson, Eckersley. Front: Matthews, Taylor, Mortensen, Sewell and Robb.

ENGLAN

OF REG

IKE most of his fellow professionals, Jimmy Dickinson was by now aware that the English were no longer masters of the game. England were, however, still the one nation that most countries longed to beat. The Continentals had shown sufficient skill and imagination to suggest that British football had fallen behind Europe at least. As the 1953-4 season unfolded, dramatic confirmation of that truth lay only weeks away.

A traumatic international year for England coincided with the Football Association's 90th anniversary and in October 1953 this was marked by a match against a FIFA XI, its players drawn from six nations. The game was drawn 4-4 but only a late penalty-kick by Alf Ramsey rescued England. Dickinson wondered at the fascinating brand of football played by the Europeans that day as they settled down to play their short-passing 'possession' game. Moves of nine and ten passes were quite normal and the understanding between the FIFA players was all the more remarkable for the fact that they had come together as a team, only for that one game.

Dickinson and Billy Wright had played alongside each other in the England half-back line on more than 30 occasions. Now they faced the challenge of the Hungarian national team. There was a fair degree of confidence in the England camp that damp, misty November afternoon. After all, England had never lost at home to a foreign side, except to the Republic of Ireland whose team was comprised mostly of Football League players. Yet these 'Magical Magyars' in their plum-coloured shirts stunned the 100,000 crowd with a brand of football which seemed to be from another planet.

The football world was astonished by the ease of the Hungarians' victory. They won 6-3 and, as Dickinson admitted later, might easily have reached double-figures, so overrun were he and his fellow defenders. The Hungarians, with footballers like Puskas, Kocsis, Bozsik and the deep-lying centre-forward Hidegkuti, showed skills and a tactical approach which were unknown in English football. In later years Dickinson would recount how the Hungarians could trap the ball on their chests, thighs and insteps — and, to his amazement, often in the tightest situations, where a British player would have opted for safety first.

The way, for instance, Puskas evaded a tackle by Billy Wright by pulling back the ball from the path of the

'S TIME ONING

England captain with the sole of his left boot and then swivelling to crash a shot into the roof of the net, typified the Hungarians' complete mastery. One commentator likened Wright's attempted tackle on Puskas to "a fire-engine going to the wrong fire".

The manner of the defeat challenged Jimmy Dickinson's whole coaching philosophy. Portsmouth Football Club, amongst others, also took notice and Eddie Lever re-examined his training methods. For too long, League clubs had gone in for tedious training stints of lapping, jogging and cross-country running. Now there were attempts to introduce some aspects of the European game. By the end of the 1950s, fresh jargon from abroad was to creep into the game with the wave of 'new thinking'. England clearly had a lot of catching-up to do. In mitigation there were too many inexperienced players in the England side which faced Hungary that day. Injuries affected team plans and the selectors had to look to Spurs' amateur winger, George Robb, to solve one of their problems.

Defeat by Hungary — the first England international to be televised live in Britain — shocked the nation's football fans and reduced England's World Cup aspirations to rubble. Dickinson, like others unlucky enough to have been exposed to the Hungarian magic, was fearful that his international place was in jeopardy with the World Cup Finals in Switzerland only seven months away.

Months of waiting were rewarded the following April when he was selected for the match at Hampden, a game which was also the final match in the British qualifying group for the World Cup. Only four players survived the Hungary experience — Gil Merrick in goal, half-backs Wright and Dickinson and, inevitably, Stanley Matthews. It was a relief for Dickinson that a fresh England team appeared to be constructed around him but, although Scotland were beaten 4-2, it was an unconvincing victory. Roger Byrne, the Manchester United captain, earned his first cap along with Ron Staniforth of Huddersfield Town and Harry Clarke of Spurs, but Dickinson found it difficult to co-ordinate his play with the newcomers. In addition he found his Pompey colleague Jackie Henderson, at centre-forward for Scotland, a lively opponent with his usual speed and aggression.

As in 1950, England embarked on a two-match preparation for the World Cup Finals, just a month before the competition began. Jimmy Dickinson would have welcomed a break at home in Alton and the chance to spend some precious time with Ann, now his regular companion, who was working at Alton General Hospital.

Dickinson was pleased to have Peter Harris in the England party which left for Eastern Europe. The first match of the short trip brought a 1-0 defeat at the hands of the muscular Yugoslavians. One week later there was a real catastrophe. Many people doubted the wisdom of a return match with Hungary in Budapest, arguing that it hardly seemed the best way to prepare England's players for the World Cup. Their worst fears were justified and Hungary crushed England 7-1, their heaviest defeat to date. Peter Harris, Pompey's flying winger, had the great misfortune to make his England return after years in the international wilderness. Both he and Dickinson were disappointed in Walter Winterbottom's plans and Harris found himself having to undertake a marking and tackling assignment in midfield, a role totally alien to him. He and Dickinson were overwhelmed by wave upon wave of Hungarian attacks. For Harris it was a last chance to impress and, in the face of competition from Matthews and Finney, he missed selection for the World Cup squad.

England set off for the Finals in Switzerland. For so many years the unofficial 'kings' of football, they were now poorly regarded. Dickinson, though, was optimistic, saying, "Our chances are better than they were at Rio." Certainly, England's historical position in the game still made them the one country that all the others wanted to beat, even though they were no longer masters of the football world. Winterbottom did not believe in keeping players away from their families for longer than necessary. As a result, the England squad were the last to arrive in Switzerland, only two and a half days before their first match.

Jimmy Dickinson, at 29 years of age and with 35 caps to his name, was about to compete in his second World Cup series. The squad, with an average age of 29 making it the oldest England would ever send to the Finals, made themselves comfortable in the picturesque town of Lucerne. For their opening match, against Belgium in Basle, they were acutely aware that the nation's eyes were on them through the newly-created Eurovision facility which transmitted the games live to British television viewers. Television would become a potent force in world football, not always for the better.

The spectators might have found the game between England and Belgium an entertaining spectacle but it ended in disappointment for England after they squandered a two-goal advantage and allowed the Belgians to draw 4-4 after extra-time. Dickinson battled to compensate for a shaky display by the Luton Town centre-half Syd Owen and goalkeeper Gil Merrick also had a disappointing game. Extra-time produced another goal for Lofthouse but Belgium snatched a draw when Dickinson's head deflected a free-kick past Merrick for an own-goal. The defensive performance was considered naive by the Press and *The Times* lamented, "England were like those rare children of light who can pass through any experience protected by a sheath of impenetrable innocence." Significantly, Billy Wright spent the closing minutes at centre-half with Owen

Above: Wright, Dickinson and Ramsey (on line) watch anxiously as Merrick tips a Hungary shot round the post at Wembley, November 1953.

limping from cramp. Wright would remain at centre-half for five distinguished years, extending his international career to become the first England player to earn over 100 caps.

Three days later, on a hot afternoon in Berne, England

Opposite: The England party arrive in Berne for the 1954 World Cup Finals.

Hungary forward Kocsis heads towards the England goal as Dickinson arrives to cover.

opponents and had just destroyed Scotland 7-0. After 40 minutes, however, England were more than holding their own with the score at 1-1. Then Dickinson headed away a free-kick but succeeded only in directing the ball to the Uruguayan forward Varela, who shot past Merrick from 25 yards. Shortly after the interval the brilliant Schiaffino, who Dickinson had found difficult to contain, scored a third and the technical superiority of the South Americans began to tell. Walter Winterbottom recalls that, although Dickinson took the defeat in his usual quiet manner, the Pompey man was deeply upset by his mistake at a crucial time in the game. The sensitive Portsmouth captain had always been inclined to worry if his performance dipped below its usual immaculate best.

Despite the 4-2 defeat, England had given one of their more creditable World Cup performances to date and Jimmy Dickinson, in his last appearance in the tournament, had maintained his own international status. While the rest of the England party flew home, Dickinson, with Billy Wright and Walter Winterbottom, stayed on for the last eight days to watch the remainder of the competition.

Dickinson, who had never really enjoyed watching the game, saw the finest football match he had ever witnessed when Hungary, the favourites, beat Uruguay, the holders, 4-2 after extra-time in the semi-final in Lausanne. The three men were stunned by the high technical skills displayed during one of the greatest games in soccer history. After Germany's surprise win in the Final, Dickinson, Wright and Winterbottom returned home convinced that England would have to review their whole attitude to the game.

Lever had noted some of the more successful tactics and methods and he introduced new ideas to Fratton Park. They probably contributed to Pompey's good season in 1954-5, a campaign in which Dickinson was to suffer a new experience for him, that of sitting on the sidelines nursing an injury. In the meantime, he was glad to return from Switzerland to the peace of Alton and thoughts of marriage to Ann.

faced Switzerland in their second and concluding Pool match before a crowd of 60,000. At the end of a dreary match, which England won 2-0, Dickinson was exhausted but happy that the quarter-finals had been reached. There had been much hostility from the English Press corps and it was upsetting to read some of the comments in the available English newspapers. Typical was, "England, in a world sense, represent a Third Division side that has found its way into the last eight of the FA Cup."

In the six days before the quarter-final there was time for Pompey manager Eddie Lever to fly to Switzerland in an attempt to find the key to the success of opponents Uruguay, the World Cup holders. Lever watched them in training and saw a variety of work designed to produce fitness and stamina but, above all, mastery of the ball.

Uruguay, who had won all three World Cup tournaments for which they had entered, were formidable

THE severe ankle injury which caused Jimmy Dickinson to miss the start of the 1954-5 season, then another four months through to March 1955, was not the only threat to his England place. At first his absence was covered by Ray Barlow from West Brom and then Bill Slater from Wolves, but the emergence of Duncan Edwards, who made his full England debut at left-half against Scotland, was enough to put the Pompey player in the shadows of international selection. Preparations for the match were marred by the serious training accident to Len Phillips who was due to play at right-half. The injury ended his international career and later his First Division days.

Dickinson had already missed three matches when Edwards, at 18 probably the youngest English player to win a full international cap, made his mark in the 7-2 hammering of Scotland. Edwards, the greatest of Manchester United's 'Busby Babes', was already a mature footballer both in physical strength and skill. He was immediately the new folk-hero of English football, "striding the Wembley pitch like a colossus," according to one newspaper.

Edwards was certainly no babe. He went on to gain 18 full caps and at the time of his death at Munich, although only 21, he was playing like a veteran and probably England's future captain. Winterbottom recalls that Edwards, quite simply, had more potential than any other player he had come across in 20 years' coaching. Full of confidence, the Manchester United star had no weaknesses and, according to Winterbottom, he was the hardest kicker of a football in the game, a fact apparently established by a scientific test.

After a disappointing season, during which he suffered injury and a decline in his personal form, Jimmy Dickinson received a boost when the FA announced his inclusion in the England party for the close-season trip to France, Spain and Portugal, for what was to prove his last Continental tour. He was still held in sufficient esteem by Winterbottom to warrant a place in the squad, but sat out the 1-0 defeat in Paris in the first match.

Included at right-half for a bruising, scrappy draw against Spain, Dickinson retained his place for the last game, in Oporto, when two goals presented to the Portuguese in the last ten minutes sealed England's fate 3-1. Although unhappy to be played on the right side of the half-back line, he was none the less pleased to have extended his international career.

England were now beginning to look suspect against even mediocre sides. A struggle to beat the part-timers of Denmark in Copenhagen, before the Danish king and queen, underlined England's poor form at that time. The Press were united in their opinion that Dickinson was 'indispensable' as an able and experienced lieutenant of

Dickinson is joined by the young Bill Foulkes and Stanley Matthews in training before the match against Northern Ireland, November 1954, in which he did not play.

76

PARENT

Billy Wright, who this time had a mediocre match. The same month, in Cardiff, Wales scored their first victory over England for 17 years, thanks mainly to John Charles and his command in the air. England wins over Northern Ireland and Spain flattered to deceive but the Ireland match at Wembley saw an impressive debut by right-half Ronnie Clayton of Blackburn, the latest young challenger to the half-back positions, along with Bill McGarry of Huddersfield and Ron Flowers of Wolves.

The final match of the Home Internationals was once again to settle the Championship and England's 1-1 draw at Hampden Park meant that the Championship was shared between the four countries for the first time. Dickinson was moved to right-half again to accommodate Edwards and again the Pompey man gave one of his best England performances for the historic gathering of the clans. Most of the 134,000 crowd were acclaiming Scotland's first victory on their native soil for 19 years when Fulham's Johnny Haynes scored a last-minute equaliser. Hampden fell silent as Jimmy Dickinson left the field after providing superb support for man-of-the-match Haynes. Dickinson would have guessed that day that this would be his last appearance against the Scots at Hampden, where he had enjoyed some magnificent battles and usually displayed his best form. In his five matches against Scotland, Dickinson had never been on the losing side. No wonder he had so many happy memories of games against England's oldest football enemy.

He ended Pompey's last match of the season, against Manchester City, limping from an ankle injury which did not mend in time for the first visit of the colourful Brazilians to Wembley. The same injury prevented him joining England's summer Continental tour and the emergence of Second Division Blackburn's Clayton seemed to herald the end of the long-serving wing-half combination of Wright and Dickinson. Wright was now at centre-half and Clayton and Edwards were the new young lions. The Press still awaited the return to fitness of Pompey's mercurial

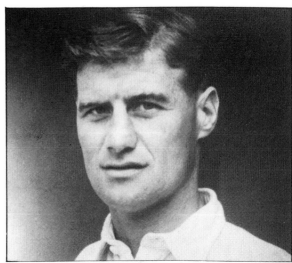
The proud international

Len Phillips but the wait was to be in vain.

The summer tour was a success, ending in an astonishing 3-1 success over the World Cup holders, West Germany in Berlin. When Dickinson was overlooked for the opening international of 1956-7, it really did look like the end of the road. It was a pleasant surprise, then, when he was included in the England party in the unaccustomed role of travelling reserve for the Wales match in November 1956. When Edwards suffered an ankle injury in the previous Saturday's League match, Jimmy Dickinson found himself recalled to the team and his performance in England's 3-1 win showed that he still had something to offer. He retained his place for Yugoslavia's first visit to Wembley two weeks later and Edwards had to settle for being the reserve. England's 3-0 win was due in no small measure to Dickinson's control of the brilliant

Dickinson watches as Sillett heads clear against Spain in Madrid, May 1955.

Jimmy Dickinson is in close attendance as Gil Merrick snatches the ball from the feet of Wales' Reg Davies at Wembley.

Yugoslav forward, Vukas. Vukas showed flair with his close dribbling and change of direction but still failed to draw Dickinson into a false position or tackle.

One week later England embarked on another World Cup qualifying campaign, a ten-match unbeaten run over 14 months stretching behind them. For Jimmy Dickinson it was his third World Cup series but the game against Denmark, at Molineux, on 5 December 1956, was also his last international appearance. His chance came when Johnny Haynes was declared unfit and Duncan Edwards was pushed forward to inside-left. Fifty-five thousand fans saw England beat the Danes 5-2, with a hat-trick by Tommy Taylor of Manchester United and two blistering goals from his club-mate Edwards. For Dickinson it was not a conspicuous 'swan-song'. The England defence had some uneasy moments and only Edwards' virtuosity and Taylor's finishing separated the Danish youngsters from their English opponents. It was certainly not the most auspicious occasion for Jimmy Dickinson's 48th and final cap.

Further international appearances were virtually eliminated after Dickinson switched to centre-half for Pompey a month later. Pompey's desperate need was enough to persuade him to forgo his international career, although he was well aware that it would signal the end of his England days.

Billy Wright was now established as England's centre-half, but the Munich air disaster one year later claimed the life of the magnificent Edwards. The 1958 World Cup preparations were shattered by the deaths by Byrne, Taylor, David Pegg and Edwards but it was too late for Jimmy Dickinson to make a international comeback.

The veteran Wolves wing-half Bill Slater had the edge over Dickinson, largely by virtue of playing in the successful Wolves team of the era, while Dickinson struggled to shore up a shaky Pompey defence from centre-half.

Jimmy Dickinson inevitably missed international involvement and his England caps meant a lot to him. He summed up his feelings, "How do I prefer to play for England? I've played it long out of defence, chipped out of defence, carried it out of defence and if I couldn't see anyone to give it to, then I belted it out of sight. In this game you do what you're told. And you have to do a lot of things to win an England cap."

Although he would not admit it, the loss of the international fees — which, for many years, were £50 per match — was a financial blow. Before the abolition of the maximum wage in 1961, the fees were a welcome and regular part of Jimmy Dickinson's income and he would not have wanted to lose these supplements to his modest wages at Fratton Park.

He would miss his close friend Billy Wright and his valued relationship with Walter Winterbottom. For his part, Winterbottom fondly remembers the honest nature of the Portsmouth legend and his quite, circumspect behaviour at all times. For many years Dickinson had been a close lieutenant of the England manager, who had valued his opinions and the fact that he was a trusted confidant.

Dickinson would miss seeing and pitting his skills against the best players in the world. Yet, despite all the foreign stars in contention, he was adamant about his choice of the most complete footballer he had ever seen. "Wilf Mannion, the Middlesbrough and England inside-forward, was the best. He was both an outstanding individual player and very much a team man. Wilf was so elusive that you could be standing with him and the next second he had slipped four or five yards away." Mannion invariably provided Dickinson with almost insurmountable problems at club level, with his mixture of skill, confidence and audacity. Further afield, Dickinson would remember the Hungarian Kocsis from those defeats of 1953 and 1954. "He always seemed to blend perfectly with the players around him. He was almost the complete footballer'.

International football also left Dickinson with some amusing memories. He was not one of those players who gave way to superstition and so he was particularly intrigued by the antics of Manchester United's Henry Cockburn, who liked to pin a 'lucky' black cat emblem inside his shirt before taking the field. On one occasion the emblem found its way straight into the England laundry basket after an international and it had to be parcelled up and sent to him by train, in time for United's next League game, after an urgent plea from Old Trafford. The superstitions in the England camp reached farcical proportions when only seven players lined up in the Wembley tunnel before one game. It transpired that the others were still in the dressing-room, each one vying to be last in line, as they were when playing for their clubs.

Now all this was over for Jimmy Dickinson, for so long a household name in domestic football and a man who had enjoyed a fine reputation wherever he had played in the world. It had taken the once-in-a-lifetime talent of Duncan Edwards to depose him. Dickinson withdrew from the international scene, satisfied that in every one of his 48 full appearances he had given his best, even though he had seen some of the blackest days in England's football history.

Ahead of him lay Pompey's imminent slide into relegation and with it life in the lower divisions and a playing career extended to more years than he could possibly have imagined. The day would dawn when, of all those great footballers of the 1940s and 1950s, only Jimmy Dickinson would remain on the field of play.

Duncan Edwards, the heir apparent, watches as Billy Wright heads clear from Northern Ireland centre-forward Jimmy Jones in Belfast.

Desk-bound after all those active years.

BACKROOM BOY

WITH his role in public relations now on a full-time basis Jimmy Dickinson was encouraged by George Smith to get as close as possible to the supporters and increase active interest in the club. To this end he endeavoured to meet people in the social and business worlds in and around the city and, of course, he was invariably a welcome visitor by virtue of his name and public image. In truth, Dickinson was never sufficiently extrovert or outgoing, or in current parlance 'dynamic', to meet the needs or profile of a modern public relations or marketing man.

The switch to a desk-bound job, with the occasional trips out in the town, needed some adjustment after the hurly-burly of the dressing-room, the rigours of training and the tensions of match-day. Dickinson compensated on the playing front by turning out regularly on a Sunday afternoon for the Ex-Portsmouth FC Professionals team. He was to have a long and happy association with this team which was formed and managed by the enthusiastic Len Curtis and played matches in aid of local charities. Indeed, Dickinson's first appearance was the day after his traumatic last match at Northampton, so keen was he to help out. The charity matches, often played on local

recreation grounds and even once in a farmer's field with accompanying cow-pats, enabled Dickinson to put something back into the game — as if he really needed to — by helping to raise hundreds of pounds each year. There was never any question, however, of this veteran appearing with a middle-age spread and going through the motions to feed a crowd's nostalgia. There was still the same pride and commitment in his play and general fitness as he indulged himself in his love of playing even before a few hundred spectators.

In those early months of his new job, the Fratton Park organisation was working hard on the events which would contribute to Dickinson's Testimonial Fund, a fund which was to eventually close at a figure in excess of £7,000. The highlight was an evening of football featuring two matches, the first between an Old England International XI, which included such legendary players as Matthews, Finney and Wright, and a full Portsmouth Championship XI. The second game was between the then current Portsmouth team and West Ham United, fresh from their European Cup-winners' Cup Final success. A crowd of 19,000 made it a gala night and they took their chance to give Jimmy Dickinson a tumultuous farewell.

Dickinson's retirement had coincided with the scrapping of the club's reserve and youth teams on Smith's recommendation. In that new season Pompey operated with a single side selected from a 16-man squad. As always, the club was beset by financial worries and it was a controversial decision but one which was felt necessary to reduce the mounting bank overdraft. Dickinson was uneasy about the move and looked back on it in later years as being at the root of Portsmouth Football Club's stagnation. He commented, "We subsequently found it difficult to compete financially with the Arsenals and Manchester Uniteds in the transfer market and, at the same time, we were not producing our own players either, so the move proved to be a disaster."

Dickinson's replacement at centre-half, Vince Radcliffe, broke his leg early in the season and his replacement, Frank Haydock from Charlton, cost a £20,000 fee which Pompey could barely afford. While the team languished in mid-table for that season and the following campaign, Dickinson was employed in various activities drumming up interest and finance, particularly on match-days. These ranged from a Ladies Day, where wives and girlfriends of supporters sat in the stand as guests, to a Family Day where supporters left their children in the care of Ann Dickinson and her volunteer helpers. In addition to launching a fund-raising 'armchair bingo', Dickinson could be found most weeks sitting on a football forum with Smith and the new assistant PRO, John Phelps, at locations throughout the area. At that particular time 20 years ago, all these activities were somewhat revolutionary and, indeed, they stand in stark contrast to the club's lack of public contact in recent years.

After Dickinson had recovered from the loss of his mother Alice, at the age of 74, at the Alton family home where he had been brought up and where she had outlived her husband by some 26 years, he returned from his family holiday in the summer of 1968, to be offered a new job at Fratton Park. After the resignation of the long-time club secretary, Reg Mulcock, the job was filled on a temporary basis for 18 months and then accepted by Dickinson with some enthusiasm. The public relations could be left in the good hands of the ambitious John Phelps who had now served his apprenticeship.

Dickinson was largely unfamiliar with the demands of his new job and, like most players, he had only a vague idea of the tasks and responsibilities involved in the secretary's work. Happily, he was eased into the position with the help of the vastly experienced and loyal assistant-secretary Leslie Spink. Dickinson had an unusual background for such a position. Most football club secretaries have qualifications in law or accountancy and are recruited from the business world or, at least, have learnt the job by junior service in the club office.

Dickinson was one of the very few professional footballers to convert to secretary and, of course, he had no business background in or out of football. It is a tribute to his intelligence and resourcefulness — the exercise of his brain during his playing days had been limited largely to the complexities of the *Daily Telegraph* crossword — that he was able to absorb and then undertake the accounting and administrative demands of the job with little apparent difficulty.

Like any company secretary, Dickinson would be involved in the bookkeeping and accounting aspects with responsibility for the payment of wages and PAYE. He would, amongst other duties, draw up and register players' contracts, register share transfers and administer the sale and issue of season tickets. On alternate weeks he and the staff would work a six-day week to fall in with the home match-day tasks. A long day would involve him with the supervision of turnstile operators and stewards, reception and accommodation at the ground of the Press, visiting team's directors and the referee and linesmen. Once the match had started, the receipts had to be collected and transfer to the bank arranged.

Ron Tindall – a firm friend as the new manager.

When the match was over Dickinson, as the club's most famous name, would be expected to socialise in the boardroom for an hour or so. He never found that aspect easy by virtue of his still retiring nature, but it would be made easier if, as often happened, he encountered old friends from his international or club playing days and had a chance to reminisce.

Dickinson enjoyed being 'his own boss' and became completely immersed in the job. His interest in contemporary football waned rapidly, however. He derived a good measure of job satisfaction from his heavy workload in the service of his beloved Portsmouth FC — almost a labour of love and more than just a job of work. His philosophy was summed up in these remarks, "You could say I have the best of both worlds because I am close to football without the worries. I find the job satisfying, it interests me and keeps me in touch with the game which has been my life."

After Dickinson's first three years in the job, George Smith relinquished the team managership, moved 'upstairs' to the role of general manager and handed over to Ron Tindall who had been groomed for the job. Tindall, like Dickinson, was a thoughtful, serious and seemingly diffident man. The two men, with the same sporting interests in cricket and golf, were firm friends. Smith had noted Tindall's leadership qualities as a player who was a reliable performer without the charisma or brilliance that catches the headlines.

Tindall adopted an industrial management technique to chart his course but, although Dickinson was impressed by the intense 'management by objectives', the massive improvement hoped for in the club's position did not come. At this stage the team had not been washed back into the Third Division but they were barely afloat in the Second.

Dickinson, as a taste of things to come, was increasingly involved in cost-cutting as the club were still hampered by a cash deficit and the consequent tight limit on transfers. Dickinson would, for example, organise cheap coach travel for the team to away matches and arrange ground cleaning by the club's own staff rather than contractors. Nevertheless, the reserve and youth teams had been reinstated but by this time Smith had retired and, after the departure of Phelps, the continuing drive to integrate the club into the community was in the hands of the young graduate, Alan Sefton.

Pompey's financial worries seemed to have disappeared with the arrival of John Deacon as chairman, coupled with his massive injection of capital as the club approached its 75th anniversary in 1973-4. This was evidenced by the major purchases of Ron Davies from Southampton, Paul Went from Fulham and Peter Marinello from Arsenal, among other recruits, with the prime intention of a quick return to the First Division. Public interest was high but the team, assembled at such great cost, fell short of expectations. As Dickinson put it, "We had some good players alright, but they really did not seem to want to play for us." Deacon had by now appointed John Mortimore as manager and Tindall became general manager, a role which further cemented his close relationship with Dickinson.

Mortimore did not bring the immediate success demanded and early the following season, 1974-5, he was replaced by Ian St John, the former Liverpool and Scotland forward who had been managing Motherwell. St John came on a personal recommendation to Deacon from Bill Shankly. St John arrived with a rush of enthusiasm and Dickinson was initially impressed with his energy and complete confidence in his own ability. The two men were complete opposites but even Dickinson could not have foreseen the immense problems which St John was to face and which would lead to his downfall.

The financial stringency at the club, in stark contrast to the profligate spending one year previously, meant that the new manager worked with a small group of players and that none of the finance, promised to him on his appointment, was available for new recruits. As it transpired, St John preferred to use the younger up-and-coming players and believed that the Pompey club should draw its strength from local schools and clubs, producing its own players.

As the bank overdraft grew menancingly under the strain of the massive wage-bill, expended on players who were not producing success, Jimmy Dickinson was prominent in the now desperate efforts to find fresh sources of income. Behind the scenes Dickinson was the only constant figure as Tindall departed together with a string of six directors in nine months. Beside his enormous stake in the club, chairman John Deacon was finding large sums from his own pocket to keep Pompey alive and running.

The inevitable relegation to Division Three the following season, 1975-6, had coincided with an exodus of experienced — and expensively recruited — players and with St John putting his faith in a number of young players from Ray Crawford's youth team. By September 1976 it was a cause of great concern to Dickinson that the club was clearly in desperate straits and facing extinction. He knew that the position had deteriorated to the extent that money had to be injected to meet even the most basic demands on the club. Of even more concern to him was the curtain which was being drawn publicly over the extent of the crisis.

Dickinson was finally to break the silence and take the initiative with an unauthorised statement to the local Press before the home match against Lincoln. He told them, "Quite honestly, I fear for the future of the club. I fear for our existence if something is not done. I can only say that we need people at Fratton Park tomorrow, desperately." The debts exceeded £500,000 and the chairman, who had already put £400,000 into the club, came out into the open three days later and admitted that a minimum of £25,000 had to be raised publicly in six weeks to clear the most pressing debts.

It was in such an atmosphere that Dickinson worked as secretary and, by his nature, he took the strain personally as if it were his very own livelihood at stake. He had to face players and staff who were kept waiting for their expenses, bonuses and even their wages on occasions. Even to the phlegmatic Dickinson it seemed only a matter of time before a major creditor forced payment and he and

his staff turned off the lights at Fratton Park and got the workmen to nail up the door.

With the announcement of the public appeal, Dickinson felt a weight lifted from his shoulders. "Obviously my feeling is one of relief that the public have at last been informed of the situation." A lively little businessman, Harry Garcia, was the inspiration behind the 'SOS Pompey' appeal launched by the local newspaper *The News*. The persuasive powers of Garcia, as the chairman of a committee comprising local newspaper and business-men, mobilised the support needed. The money rolled in with donations from all over the country, particularly from former Royal Navy personnel who had served in Ports-mouth. There is no doubt that Dickinson's presence at the club as central figure in the crisis and a link with the past helped tremendously as £35,000 was raised overall. The energetic and immediate response locally was evidence of the club's place in the city's affections.

With the immediate debts cleared, the worries switched to the pitch where St John had faced a daunting task in trying to produce a winning side against a background of uncertainty and player unrest. Dickinson watched from the wings as several experienced players 'crossed swords' with the abrasive St John and were left to languish in the Reserves. St John's faith in his teenagers was almost complete and he fielded up to seven recent graduates from Ray Crawford's youth team.

By the spring of 1977, Pompey were firmly in the relegation frame with the Fourth Division beckoning for the first time in the famous old club's history. St John's position, meanwhile, was becoming increasingly untenable. The month of April ended with Portsmouth in the penul-timate position with only four matches left.

The team and its supporters were in desperate need of some inspiration and a return to the unquestioning club loyalty and pride of the past. Behind-the-scenes moves were already afoot for those needs to be provided from a most unexpected source.

Top, left: A happy reunion of players from the 1950s. At back (from left): Froggatt, Rookes, Dickinson, Len Phillips, Butler, Reid, Rutter, Barnard, Clarke. Front: Ferrier, Scoular, Peter Harris, and Stephen.

Bottom, left: Mecca Loyalty Awards presentation. Back (left to right): Jack Charlton, John Trollope, Ron Harris, Roy Sproson and Dickinson. Front: Ian Callaghan, Terry Paine, and Joe Shaw.

Top, right: John Mortimore, stayed only a short while in the hot seat.

Bottom, right: Ian St John, arrived with a rush of enthusiasm.

First day as manager and a first meeting with the players. From left: Denyer, Figgins, Ellis, Mellows and Pollock.

THE JOB HE

AS Jimmy Dickinson drove down to his office on the morning of Wednesday, 4 May 1977, he would have known that this was to be one of the more eventful days in his long association with Portsmouth Football Club. In the days that had gone before, the whisper that he was about to be offered the chance to become manager had grown to near deafening proportions as Pompey's latest 'below-stairs' revolution unfolded. Dickinson would also have known that he was, almost inevitably, to be thrown a challenge that day — a challenge that he would not be able to resist or avoid.

Like everyone at the club, he was conscious of the pressure building up incessantly, week by week, upon Ian St John as the manager tried to work a miracle from slender playing resources and non-existent transfer funding. The pressure had climaxed in a home defeat by Grimsby the previous Saturday, a defeat which had been marked by the crowd's strident barracking of the manager. Ian St John's son, a ball-boy at Fratton Park that day, was reduced to tears and St John was so upset that he had offered his resignation to the board the same evening.

With three matches left, of which only one was at home, Pompey were in a perilous position. The Monday evening of that fateful week had seen the problems further increased by a 2-0 defeat at Mansfield. During a tense journey home, which took almost all the following day after the team's motor-coach broke down, St John heard on the radio that his future was to be discussed by the five-man board at a meeting the following morning.

When that board meeting, convened in mid-morning, stretched into the middle of the afternoon it was obvious that some momentous decision was forthcoming. When it came it was still a shock and possibly ill-timed at that stage of the season. St John had withdrawn his offer to resign, a decision which had been made in the heat of the moment amidst the frustration of defeat. The board were, however, upset at his outburst and suspended the manager on full pay with just under half of his five-year £12,000 per annum contract still to run.

When Jimmy Dickinson was approached by chairman John Deacon in the late afternoon and offered the manager's job on a 'temporary' basis, he simply could not bring himself to refuse. Whether he should have taken the job or not — and many with hindsight have reflected that he should not have done so — it was still a brave decision. As he said at the time, "It's probably the biggest decision I will ever make." He loved the club and could not in any way resist the call for help. He took the job, although throughout his career he had vowed that he would never become a manager. "It wasn't that I wanted the job, but I felt it was my duty to do what I could for the club which had been my life. I felt I had to. I was fed up with the way things were going. It was an easy decision to try to lead the fight against relegation. I'll know

EVER WANTED

that I've tried and that's the least anyone can do."

The board were only too aware of the need to re-establish the rapport between the club and its supporters and the appointment of the legendary figure from the glory days, with whom the public still had such great affinity, at this time of crisis was seen as a move in the right direction. A desperate need was felt for a return to the days of 'pulling together' and values which Dickinson's presence might produce both on the terraces and in the dressing-room. Possibly of more significance was the stark fact that the club simply could not afford to recruit another manager. Mortimore had still to be paid off and St John, under suspension, was still on the payroll.

Ann Dickinson did not want her husband to take the job and typically told him so. But, like many a good wife, she was prepared to support her man in any venture if he was so completely determined and committed to it. As for Dickinson's suitablity for the job at his time of life, there must be considerable doubt, looking back from this distance. By his own admission, his interest in the modern game had waned over the years. He had become only an occasional spectator and did not comprehend or enjoy the fundamental changes which had taken place in the game.

As club secretary, Dickinson had become somewhat remote from the players and had played no part in dressing-room life for some time. Many of the team were too young to have known him as a player. To them he was only a name, repeated so often on the roll of honour in the board-room. Despite this obvious generation gap, many of the players were genuinely pleased with Dickinson's appointment. Others, though, felt that it had come at the wrong time, both for the man and the club. In Dickinson's favour was his genuine devotion to the cause and also the vast and amazing goodwill which supporters had for the club and which he could harness.

Dickinson was to be a manager without a title and without a contract. Typically, he sidestepped that issue. "I wouldn't want a contract for the first year anyway, until I had proved myself." Here was the first hint that Dickinson had some ambition in the job, other than assuming the post on a stopgap basis. His intentions regarding his relationship with the players immediately became apparent when he declined to be called 'boss', as most managers have been traditionally known by their teams.

On his first full day in the job he appointed Ray Crawford, the former Ipswich and England forward, as first-team coach in place of St John's lieutenant, Billy Hunter. Crawford was an exceptional coach and had gained a good reputation in charge of Pompey's youth team. Portsmouth were eventually to reap the rewards of his efforts with the maturing of players such as Peter Denyer, Keith Viney, Chris Kamara and Steve Foster, the latter becoming an England centre-half after moving to Brighton.

At his first training session as manager, Dickinson made his philosophy clear. "All I ask of the players is that they are fair with me — I will then be fair with them." Dickinson was in complete contrast to the aggressive, dominant St John and was determined not to lose his 'Gentleman Jim' image. "I will not become a bastard. I don't think you have to swear and scream to get results. We will have discipline but you have to work with people." Out of that came a relaxed, family atmosphere at the club with Dickinson always ready to listen, particularly to experienced players who were able to give full vent to their opinions. The team was run on simple theories with no analytical approaches. Dickinson's main theme was based on the pride of wearing a Pompey shirt and the commitment owed to the supporters. If the players were looking for the archetypal manager, part-psychologist and part-master tactician, they were disappointed.

Dickinson was left with three matches to extricate the club from the threat of relegation. "I felt a little like a substitute brought on in the last five minutes to try and save the game."

The following Saturday saw Pompey earn a priceless point at Preston with a dour defensive display after Dickinson had recalled experienced defenders Phil Roberts and Billy Wilson. Their recall was even more dramatic for the fact that the two had already left the club a few days before, to see out their contracts away from Fratton Park.

The critical last home match, against already-doomed York City, simply had to be won to ensure survival. As it transpired, Pompey won easily 3-1, due largely to the combination of intense emotional support from the 14,000 crowd, who were so anxious for Dickinson to emerge as the saviour, and a woeful York team which was swept aside without difficulty. A banner in the crowd at the Milton End — 'Jim'll Fix It' — was evidence of the crowd's confidence in Dickinson's inspirational powers.

Despite defeat at Swindon, relegation was avoided by a point. Dickinson mused afterwards, "They were so desperate to succeed, it made my job easy." It was not a sentiment that he was ever to repeat. Pompey's players demanded a bonus as a reward for the dubious distinction of narrowly missing the drop to Division Four. Dickinson resisted their claims but their attitude bothered him and it was his first introduction to the materialistic outlook of the modern footballer.

Nevertheless, his hopes were high as he prepared for his first full season in the 'hot-seat'. He believed in the players at his disposal, believed that they were at least good enough to keep the club in the Third Division. It was as well he had such faith, for there was never any possibility of the manager having funds to buy new players. Despite the fact that Pompey's bank overdraft of nearly half a million pounds had been reduced to more manageable proportions, Dickinson enjoyed no more money than St John had to spend on strengthening the team. When Kamara was transferred to Swindon for £17,000 at the

Left: Chairman John Deacon – Dickinson could not resist his call for help in Pompey's hour of need.
Right: The long walk to the dressing room with an increasingly worried look.

start of the season, the incoming fee went towards paying off the debts. Two free-transfer signings from Southampton — goalkeeper Steve Middleton and striker Bobby Stokes, the goalscoring hero of the 1976 FA Cup Final — were secured but both were disappointments and neither fulfilled Dickinson's hopes.

Initially Dickinson trusted his players and never doubted their character and commitment. In truth, he was sadly mistaken and the extent and nature of the problems which he had inherited were to become very plain to him as the 1977-8 season unfolded. An early success in the second round of the League Cup, when First Division Leicester City were beaten, only flattered to deceive. Shattering defeats at Shrewsbury, where Portsmouth went down 6-1, and at home to Tranmere, who won 5-2 after Pompey led 2-0 at half-time, soon put them in the relegation zone and left the hapless Dickinson facing a huge task in overcoming the handicap of such a poor squad of players. Only Steve Foster, converted so masterfully to centre-half by St John, and David Kemp, the crowd's favourite, were 'saleable commodities'.

The team's inconsistency baffled Dickinson and when Ray Crawford, who had been solely responsible for training, was dismissed for disciplinary reasons, the 53-year-old manager was forced out on to the training ground. Happily, this became a rare occurrence after the senior players, particularly Eoin Hand, organised the sessions. It was, though, clearly a most unsatisfactory arrangement.

The pressures were building up and this was evidenced by Dickinson's public displays of emotions which would have been totally alien to him earlier in the job. Then he had shown his usual philosophical acceptance of the fates when they were unkind. Now the post-match briefings to the Press began to reflect the torments and the anxieties — "I was bloody ashamed.....I felt embarassed having to watch it." These were not just normal, professional opinions, they matched the reactions of the club's most dedicated supporters. Unfortunately, Jimmy Dickinson's nature meant that he found it impossible to reproach or verbally attack the players where it counted — to their faces in the dressing-room.

He aged visibly and his friends noticed a grey, worn look as he took even more comfort from his pipe. In the desperate position in which Portsmouth Football Club found itself, Dickinson clearly had no answers to the multiple on-field problems and lacked a management team to share the blows.

By the end of October 1977, Pompey had won only two matches and were in 23rd position in the Third Division with a ponderous and porous defence. Three months into the season Dickinson's frustrations were evident when he launched a scathing attack on his players at the club's annual meeting. He told the gathering, "Certain members of my staff do not have enough character and guts and this means that I must look for people who will provide these qualities for us."

The strain was mercifully relieved when, at the end of January 1978, the resolute, straight-talking Scotsman, Frank Burrows, was recruited from Swindon as first-team coach. Dickinson conceded, "I can't spend all my time running around at training but if I was ten years younger, then I wouldn't need a coach." The two men struck up an instant rapport and, ultimately, Burrows was to become the sort of inspirational figure to which Dickinson could never quite aspire, despite his many fine qualities.

Dickinson could now become almost the 'figurehead'. It was a role which suited his disposition and he was happy to leave the tactics, training and motivation to the honest, hard-working Burrows. After raising cash by selling the goalscoring David Kemp to Carlisle United, the pair began a hectic spell of transfer market activity in a bid to halt the slide towards relegation. The recruitment of Steve Piper from Brighton, Jimmy McCaffery from Huddersfield Town and the much-travelled Colin Garwood from Colchester had little immediate effect. In the last two months of the season only three matches were won and Pompey were never out of bottom place.

Dickinson summed up the disastrous season succinctly. " We went down partly through lack of money and partly because some of the players had been involved for too long with a losing team. Some of them did not have the character to do anything about it. I was kidded by the fact that we had managed to stay up last season — I thought we had the players who would fight for us."

Portsmouth's drop into the Fourth Division for the first time was a bitter pill for Dickinson and the loyal supporters to swallow and chairman John Deacon's dreams of a return to the First Division, when he came to power five years previously, seemed desperately unreal. The pressure on the manager was increased by the demand from all quarters that, for the sake of pride if nothing else, the name of Portsmouth Football Club be lifted from the depths of the Football League forthwith.

After recruiting the experienced Peter Mellor and Steve Davey from Hereford United, Pompey marked the new season with an opening-day home defeat against Bradford City, followed by defeat at York City. By the time of the next away match, at Hartlepool, Pompey faced the prospect of appearing in 92nd and last place in the Football League. It was an ignominy averted when the team scraped a draw in the last few minutes at the Victoria Ground.

After striker Jeff Hemmerman had been bought from Port Vale and Jim McIlwraith from Bury, there were reports that Deacon was exercising control of scouting and signing of players. Although the rumour was denied, the feeling persisted that Dickinson had subrogated some of his duties to the chairman. Dickinson shrugged it off. "Obviously, where there's a bit of money involved the chairman will have a say as to whether we spend it or not."

With the combination of Dickinson's gentle persuasion and Burrows' ferocious demands, the team suddenly found some colour in their cheeks and a six-match unbeaten run was aided by a flurry of goals from Colin Garwood. That run, in November 1978, earned Dickinson the 'Fourth Division Manager of the Month Award'. He seemed to have earned his spurs and Pompey's supporters, always so eager to return to Fratton Park at the first signs of any revival, swelled attendances to encouraging levels. When the team went to the top of the table in the first week of the New Year, hopes of a promotion season were high and Dickinson's collection of bargain-buys, free-transfer signings and six locally-produced players seemed capable of giving him some joy.

As it quickly transpired, however, a weather-interrupted period led to the side inexplicably losing its rhythm and, after a couple of defeats, Pompey were in danger of falling away from the promotion pack. A televised home defeat at the hands of promotion rivals Grimsby Town — after two howling errors by the normally reliable Billy Wilson — proved crucial and, as the season's run-in approached, it was becoming clear that this was not to be Pompey's year after all.

The reality of football management at the lowest level came home to Dickinson early in March that year. Pompey visited the soccer outpost of Halifax and a crowd of only 1,741 saw them stumble to another defeat after fundamental errors and a display which lacked spirit. When a small band of Pompey supporters, who had made the long journey to Yorkshire and who stood in front of the stand where Dickinson sat, turned to him and vented their frustrations, he was clearly shocked. It was the first time that he had experienced any vitriolic comment, let alone criticism, in his long career with the club — and it hurt.

The strain was beginning to tell and Ann Dickinson was conscious of her husband's increased lassitude at home. He was also increasingly reluctant to put in the mileage up and down the country to take in the games so necessary to keep a football club manager in touch.

Another dip into the transfer market — Derek Showers from Bournemouth and Steve Bryant from Northampton — was an attempt to stimulate the team but the purchase of inside-forward Showers proved a desperately unhappy affair and led to Dickinson criticising a section of Pompey's supporters. The fans did not take to Showers from the start and wasted no time in letting him know. The callous treatment meted out to the newcomer clearly upset his manager. After one particularly vocal attack on Showers throughout a home match, Dickinson turned on the fans during his post-match Press conference, telling the assembled scribes, "I don't often get angry but I was very, very angry."

Football has few winners at management level and Dickinson had suffered the pain of relegation to Division Four and now the failure to achieve a quick return to better days. 'Nice guys never win anything' is a maxim that has caused much damage in sport; it seemed to be true of Jimmy Dickinson, who never possessed the ruthless attitude, however masked, which it seems is essential for managerial success in so competitive a game. Certainly, he never enjoyed or relished the ultimate responsibility for team performances. Billy Wright, such a close friend of Dickinson and himself the model of a disciplined club player, was a most easy-going manager of Arsenal — and the least effective in that great club's recent history at the time of his resignation.

Jimmy Dickinson was a physically fit man when the

job of managing Portsmouth had been thrust on him. Now, almost two years later, he was exhausted by the rigours of watching — and suffering — poor playing performances which were outside his direct physical control; by the long working hours which every football manager must keep; and by having to concern himself ceaselessly about his players. No matter how tense a footballer may become before a match, sheer involvement in the game relieves his anxieties. Dickinson, like most managers, was very much the frustrated player, watching from the sidelines. Once the first whistle sounded he could do little or nothing to alter the course of events. For a man who had been able to shape a match during his playing days, it must have been desperately difficult to sit and watch helplessly.

As Pompey began their run-in, the sense of anti-climax was acute and the feeling in the city was one of dismay at the prospect of at least another season in the lower reaches of the League. The father-figure, who embodied the hopes of the club and its supporters, took it all personally.

Opposite: Frank Burrows – such a relief at his appointment

Below: Ray Crawford, the track-suited assistant

THE LAST DAYS

IT had been, in football parlance, 'an absolute cracker' and Jimmy Dickinson was elated. Not only had a valuable point been earned by the 1-1 draw, but it had also been a good performance. On that Friday night, 30 March 1979 at Barnsley's Oakwell ground, the Portsmouth team had shown the passion and character demanded of them in an exciting, pulsating match. The spirit in the team was good and had been fostered by the time spent together at a Barnsley hotel after the match at Bradford the previous Wednesday. Dickinson, Burrows and the players had enjoyed a day out in Leeds on the Thursday, when they had arranged a tour of the magnificent Leeds United stadium at Elland Road.

At last Dickinson could see some progress. There was light at the end of the tunnel of darkness which had enveloped much of his managerial career to date. The players were feeling quite pleased with themselves in the Oakwell dressing-room and there was the usual post-match chaos with happy, half-dressed footballers sipping tea and bumping into one another on the way to and from the showers and bath. The manager had rushed down from his seat in the directors' box and perched himself precariously on the skip into which dirty boots and shirts had just been thrown. He barely had time to mention that he did not feel well before collapsing on the dressing-room floor with a massive heart-attack.

A doctor, who was also a director of the Barnsley club, was called and within ten minutes Jimmy Dickinson was in the intensive-care unit at the local hospital. He was seriously ill and for some days the medical bulletins described his condition as 'very poorly'. He was certainly in danger of losing his life. It was a surprise to the doctors that he pulled through those early, crucial days and a tribute to his strength and the prompt attention he was given.

Ann Dickinson fondly remembers the kindness and sensitivity shown at that difficult time by Frank Burrows and by the chairman John Deacon and his wife, Joan. The Deacons drove Ann and her son, Andrew, to Barnsley the next day and arranged for them to stay in an hotel to be close to the hospital during their loved one's fight for life. Dickinson was in hospital for six weeks, slowly regaining his strength once the initial crisis was over. Although he hoped to be home, first for Easter and then

for his 54th birthday, the doctors were reluctant to release him until they were sure that he could stand the strain of the four-hour car journey home. During that six weeks he was consoled and sustained by the hundreds of letters, cards and telegrams which descended on the hospital.

When Jimmy Dickinson finally returned home for his inevitably long convalescence, Ann remembers the typically positive attitude of her husband, driven on by a determination to make a full recovery and return to his beloved Fratton Park. He was not altogether a good patient for Ann, a former nurse, and his enforced inactivity sometimes made him irritable.

By this time Dickinson had reluctantly resigned as manager and team affairs were now solely in the hands of Frank Burrows. Despite his disappointment, Dickinson naturally felt that he could not ask Pompey to keep the job open in view of his probable lengthy absence from the club. For the first time he admitted that the job had imposed an intolerable strain on him. "I suppose this attack is attributable to the pressures which I have lived with for the past few years. I'm the sort of person who tends to bottle things up and not show my feelings and I'm told that's the worst thing you can do." We shall never know just what part all that stress played in Jimmy Dickinson's fate.

We remember that the game almost broke the health of a highly-intelligent man like Joe Mercer, amongst others. Football does indeed have the power to destroy because it creates an unreal, intense atmosphere of excitement and it deals in elation and despair, bestowing these emotions upon a sensitive man at least once a week.

In his absense Dickinson was nominally appointed 'chief executive' to secure his continued employment at the club. Meanwhile, he was rightly succeeded as manager by Frank Burrows. Pompey were eighth in the table after the game at Barnsley. In the end they finished seventh with promotion just out of reach.

After a summer's rest and a holiday with the occasional gentle game of golf with his son, Jimmy Dickinson travelled down to Fratton Park at the start of the new season to find that the grandiose title of chief executive carried the duties relating to the day-to-day running of the Jimmy Dickinson Club Room, a function-room used by supporters and local social groups. John Deacon and his fellow directors were most considerate and anxious to rehabilitate Dickinson at his own pace. Thus, he was given leave to come and go as he pleased. This easy-going arrangement, which extended for some considerable time, meant that if Dickinson did not feel like travelling down to the office at any time, then no questions were asked.

Although he eventually settled into a regular daily routine with his less than onerous duties, the doctors were adamant that he would need at least a year to recover completely. Although he suffered from occasional lapses of memory, there were encouraging signs as the patient continued to progress for the remainder of that year. The following year was also negotiated without difficulty.

Pompey, meanwhile, returned to Division Three under the inspired leadership of Burrows, who was always such a strong supportive figure to Dickinson. It was a success which cheered everyone and it seemed appropriate that promotion was secured at Northampton in the last match, a repeat of that dramatic finale almost exactly 15 years earlier.

The first sign that Jimmy Dickinson's recovery was still not complete, even after two years, came when he suffered a mild stroke at home whilst shaving. A few days in hospital was the consequence. This effectively put a stop to the tennis and golf with Andrew, who had by now earned a degree at Bath University and was to continue his studies abroad before taking up a marketing appointment with a major paint manufacturer in Bristol. Andrew showed no inclination either to play or follow soccer and at university his sports were hockey and Rugby Union, a game in which he made full use of the muscular build he had inherited from his father.

In September 1982, Jimmy Dickinson suffered another heart attack. It was a major set-back and after ten days in hospital he was ordered to take life 'very, very quietly for some time to come'. Nevertheless, after six weeks of tedium at home he was tempted down to Fratton Park for what was to prove his last visit to his 'second home'. That early November evening saw Portsmouth, handily placed in fifth position in the Third Division, take on leaders Lincoln City. As a thick fog swirled eerily around the ground, Pompey played sparkling football to win 4-1. Dickinson was in good spirits and told his friends that he was hoping to resume playing tennis, albeit at a much gentler pace.

Before a week had passed, however, the sudden fatal attack at home, on that Monday afternoon of 8 November 1982, brought an end to the three-year battle for survival against the ravages of heart disease. This time there was nothing to be done and within minutes, in the lounge of the home which had so often been his sanctuary from the game's tensions and pressures, Jimmy Dickinson found that special peace.

Andrew, now 20 years of age, flew home from Santiago for the private cremation at Aldershot which was attended by family, close friends and club representatives. Later, Ann was pleased to permit a memorial service and a congregation of more than 500 ignored the driving rain to attend St Mary's Church, Fratton Road, in the centre of Portsmouth just a mile or so away from the ground. For those men who had played alongside Jimmy Dickinson and for the many people who had come in respect and admiration of a man who had given them so much pleasure, there was a particularly poignant moment when the 'Chimes', the anthem of Portsmouth Football Club throughout the post-war years and even to date, echoed hauntingly around the vast church at the end of the service.

Jimmy Dickinson, the man who, in many people's eyes, was the greatest sportsman Hampshire ever produced, was gone. We know that, in this new age, we shall never see his like again. Football gave him so much — but he gave it so much more in return.

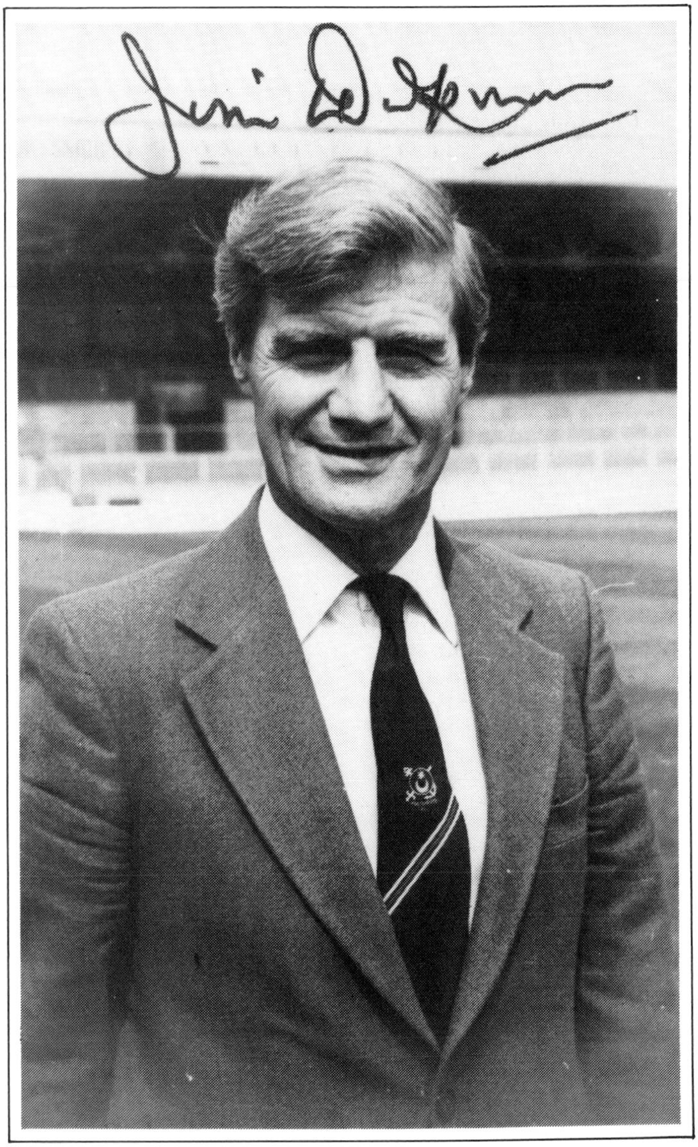

Career Milestones

April 1925: Born at Alton, Hampshire. Only son of Harry and Alice Dickinson.

January 1934: 'Discovered' by Eddie Lever, his school-teacher.

July 1939: Leaves Alton Boys School. Employed in brewery as clerk.

May 1943: Trial debut for Portsmouth v Reading.

January 1944: Signs professional forms for Portsmouth at the age of 18.

April 1944: Captains England v Scotland in Air Training Corps international.

August 1944: Begins three years' National Service in Royal Navy.

August 1946: League debut v Blackburn Rovers at Fratton Park, won 3-1.

June 1947: Bob Jackson appointed Portsmouth manager.

May 1949: Pompey win League Championship.

May 1949: International debut for England, against Norway in Oslo, won 4-1.

May 1950: Pompey win second successive League title.

June 1950: Plays in World Cup Finals in Brazil. England humiliated 1-0 by USA.

November 1950: First League goal v Charlton Athletic.

April 1951: 200th League appearance v Newcastle United at St James' Park, drew 0-0.

August 1952: Eddie Lever appointed Portsmouth manager.

November 1953: 300th League appearance v Preston North End at Fratton Park, lost 3-1.

November 1953: England 3 Hungary 6. Played in England's first home defeat by a country outside the British Isles.

June 1954: World Cup Finals in Switzerland (Scores first own-goal of career v Belgium, drew 4-4).

November 1954: Ankle injury — misses 12 matches.

June 1955: Marriage to Catherine Ann Quinton at Chawton, Alton.

October 1956: 400th League appearance v Wolves at Molineux, lost 6-0.

December 1956: 48th and last international appearance, against Denmark at Molineux, won 5-2.

May 1958: Freddie Cox appointed Portsmouth manager.

April 1959: Pompey relegated to the Second Division.

February 1959: 500th League appearance v Tottenham Hotspur at White Hart Lane, drew 4-4.

April 1961: George Smith appointed Portsmouth manager.

April 1961: Pompey relegated to the Third Division.

September 1961: 600th League appearance v Barnsley at Fratton Park, won 3-2.

May 1962: Pompey win Third Division championship.

October 1962: Birth of son, Andrew James.

November 1963: 700th League appearance v Charlton Athletic at Fratton Park, won 4-1.

June 1964: Awarded MBE in Queen's Birthday Honours List.

April 1965: 764th and final match as Pompey avoid relegation by drawing 1-1 at Northampton.

April 1965: Takes up full-time post as Portsmouth's public relations officer.

August 1968: Appointed Portsmouth FC secretary.

September 1976: 'SOS Pompey' Appeal Fund launched.

May 1977: Takes over from Ian St John as Pompey manager. Relegation avoided.

January 1978: Appointment of Frank Burrows as Portsmouth coach.

April 1978: Pompey relegated to the Fourth Division.

March 1979: Heart attack at Barnsley.

August 1979: Resigns as Portsmouth manager but appointed chief executive.

November 1982: Dies at home after another heart attack. Private cremation is followed by a memorial service.

Statistical Records

Wartime Appearances

		League		FA Cup		Total	
	Division	App	Gls	App	Gls	App	Gls
1943-44	Lge South	13	-	5	-	18	-
1944-45	Lge South	8	-	-	-	8	-
1945-46	Lge South	5	-	-	-	5	-
	Total	26	-	5	-	31	-

Post-war Appearances

		League		FA Cup		FL Cup		Total	
	Division	App	Gls	App	Gls	App	Gls	App	Gls
1946-47	One	40	-	-	-	2	-	42	-
1947-48	One	42	-	-	-	2	-	44	-
1948-49	One	41	-	-	-	5	-	46	-
1949-50	One	40	-	-	-	5	-	45	-
1950-51	One	41	2	-	-	1	-	42	2
1951-52	One	40	-	-	-	4	-	44	-
1952-53	One	40	1	-	-	2	-	42	1
1953-54	One	40	1	-	-	7	-	47	1
1954-55	One	25	-	-	-	-	-	25	-
1955-56	One	39	1	-	-	2	1	41	2
1956-57	One	42	-	-	-	2	-	44	-
1957-58	One	42	-	-	-	2	-	44	-
1958-59	One	39	2	-	-	4	-	43	2
1959-60	Two	42	-	-	-	1	-	43	-
1960-61	Two	40	-	4	-	1	-	45	-
1961-62	Three	46	-	4	-	1	-	51	-
1962-63	Two	42	-	3	-	5	-	50	-
1963-64	Two	42	-	1	-	2	-	45	-
1964-65	Two	41	-	2	-	2	-	45	-
	Totals	764	7	14	-	50	1	828	8

Full International Caps

18 May 1949	Norway	Oslo	4-1	LH
22 May 1949	France	Paris	3-1	LH
21 Sept 1949	Rep of Ireland	Goodison Park	0-2	LH
15 Oct 1949	Wales	Ninian Park	4-1	LH
15 Apr 1950	Scotland	Hampden Park	1-0	LH
14 May 1950	Portugal	Lisbon	5-3	LH
18 May 1950	Belgium	Brussels	4-1	LH
15 June 1950	Chile (WC)	Rio de Janeiro	2-0	LH
29 June 1950	USA (WC)	Belo Horizonte	0-1	LH
2 July 1950	Spain (WC)	Rio de Janeiro	0-1	LH
7 Oct 1950	N Ireland	Windsor Park	4-1	LH
15 Nov 1950	Wales	Roker Park	4-2	LH
22 Nov 1950	Yugoslavia	Highbury	2-2	LH
20 Oct 1951	Wales	Ninian Park	1-1	LH
14 Nov 1951	N Ireland	Villa Park	2-0	LH
28 Nov 1951	Austria	Wembley	2-2	LH
5 Apr 1952	Scotland	Hampden Park	2-1	LH
18 May 1952	Italy	Florence	1-1	LH
25 May 1952	Austria	Vienna	3-2	LH
28 May 1952	Switzerland	Zürich	3-0	LH
4 Oct 1952	N Ireland	Windsor Park	2-2	LH
12 Nov 1952	Wales	Wembley	5-2	LH
26 Nov 1952	Belgium	Wembley	5-0	LH
18 Apr 1953	Scotland	Wembley	2-2	LH
17 May 1953	Argentina	Buenos Aires	0-0	LH
		(Abandoned)		
24 May 1953	Chile	Santiago	2-1	LH
31 May 1953	Uruguay	Montevideo	1-2	LH
8 June 1953	USA	New York	6-3	LH
10 Oct 1953	Wales	Ninian Park	4-1	LH
21 Oct 1953	Rest of Europe	Wembley	4-4	LH
11 Nov 1953	N Ireland	Goodison Park	3-1	LH
25 Nov 1953	Hungary	Wembley	3-6	LH
3 Apr 1954	Scotland	Hampden Park	4-2	LH
16 May 1954	Yugoslavia	Belgrade	0-1	LH
23 May 1954	Hungary	Budapest	1-7	LH
17 June 1954	Belgium (WC)	Basle	4-4	LH
29 June 1954	Switzerland(WC)	Berne	2-0	LH
2 Oct 1954	Uruguay (WC)	Basle	2-4	LH
18 May 1955	Spain	Madrid	1-1	RH
22 May 1955	Portugal	Oporto	1-3	RH
2 Oct 1955	Denmark	Copenhagen	5-1	LH
22 Oct 1955	Wales	Ninian Park	1-2	LH
2 Nov 1955	N Ireland	Wembley	3-0	LH
30 Nov 1955	Spain	Wembley	4-1	LH
14 Apr 1956	Scotland	Hampden Park	1-1	RH
14 Nov 1956	Wales	Wembley	3-1	LH
28 Nov 1956	Yugoslavia	Wembley	3-0	LH
5 Dec 1956	Denmark	Molineux	5-2	LH

Playing Record   P48   W27   D11   L10   F124   A74

'B' Internationals

15 May 1949	Finland	Helsingförs	4-0	LH
18 Jan 1950	Switzerland	Hillsborough	5-0	LH
22 Feb 1950	Holland	St James' Park, Newcastle	1-0	LH

Football League Representative

22 Mar 1950	Scottish League	Ayresome Park	3-1	LH
10 Oct 1951	League of Ireland	Goodison Park	9-1	LH
31 Oct 1951	Scottish League	Hillsborough	2-1	LH
26 Mar 1951	Irish League	Belfast	9-0	LH
24 Sept 1952	Irish League	Molineux	7-1	LH
17 Mar 1953	League of Ireland	Dublin	2-0	LH
25 Mar 1953	Scottish League	Glasgow	0-1	LH
23 Sept 1953	Irish League	Belfast	5-0	LH
26 Oct 1955	Scottish League	Hillsborough	4-2	LH
7 Dec 1955	League of Ireland	Goodison Park	5-1	LH

Record Post-war Football League Appearances for One Club

1. John Trollope (Swindon Town) 770
2. **Jimmy Dickinson (Portsmouth)** **764**
3. Roy Sproson (Port Vale) 761
4. Terry Paine (Southampton) 709
5. Billy Bonds (West Ham United) 663*
6. Steve Perryman (Tottenham Hotspur) 656*
7. Ron Harris (Chelsea) 655*
8. Ian Callaghan (Liverpool) 640*
=9. Joe Shaw (Sheffield United) 629
=9. Jack Charlton (Leeds United) 629
Includes substitute appearances

'The News' Jimmy Dickinson Memorial Training Scheme

TO mark Jimmy Dickinson's outstanding contribution to the game of football a Memorial Appeal Fund was initiated by the local newspaper *The News* with the aim of furthering the interests of youth and schoolboy football in the area. It was decided, in conjunction with a local lads' league, to set up a programme of three training sessions each year for local youngsters in the school half-term holidays. The training is carried out by coaches who are recruited for the day and the Fund, which enjoys charity status, pays their fees and each day's expenses.

The Appeal Fund was launched on 10 November 1982 and as a result of the investment of the £8000-plus raised, together with subsequent donations, it has been possible to provide thousands of boys with a full day's teaching of the basic soccer skills at various centres in Hampshire. There is also a talk on Jimmy Dickinson's contribution and commitment to football and the standards he set. Each participant receives a special certificate presented by a football personality.

The continued support and publicity each half-term from *The News* keeps the name of Jimmy Dickinson and the Fund in the public eye. The fervent hope of the Trustees is that such a scheme will continue to be a fitting memorial for many years and might possibly help to produce another young talent in the manner of Dickinson to delight future generations.

Bibliography

Green, Geoffrey *Soccer in the Fifties* (Allan 1974)
Glanville, Brian *The History of the World Cup* (Faber 1984)
Rippon, Anton *Eng-land! — The Story of the National Soccer Team* (Moorland 1981)
Leatherdale, Clive *England's Quest for the World Cup* (Methven 1984)
Neasom, Cooper and Robinson *Pompey — The History of Portsmouth Football Club* (Milestone 1984)